Modern American Music

Modern American Music

From Charles Ives to the Minimalists

Otto Karolyi

cygnus arts

London **Cygnus Arts**
Madison & Teaneck **Fairleigh Dickinson University Press**

Published in the United Kingdom
by Cygnus Arts, a division of Golden Cockerel Press
16 Barter Street
London
WC1A 2AH

Published in the United States of America
by Fairleigh Dickinson University Press
Associated University Presses
440 Forsgate Drive
Cranbury
NJ 08512

First published 1996

ISBN 1 900541 00 9

British Library Cataloguing-in-Publication Data
Karolyi, Otto
  Modern American music : from Charles Ives to minimalists
  1.Music – United States – 20th century
  I.Title
  780.9'73

Library of Congress Cataloguing-in-Publication Data
Karolyi, Otto
  Modern American music : from Charles Ives to minimalists /
Otto Karolyi
      p.   cm.
  Includes bibliographical references (p.   ) and index.
  ISBN 0–8386–3725–6 (alk. paper)
    1. Music – United States – 20th century – History and criticism.
I. Title.
ML200.6K37   1996
780'.973'0904—dc20   96–9213
                                                                  CIP
                                                                  MN

Printed and Bound in Great Britain by Biddles Ltd, King's Lynn and Guildford.

To Benedikte, Julian and Emma

Contents

Foreword

THE CONTENT OF THIS BOOK IS BASED ON A LONG-standing preoccupation with American music. It goes back to those safer days in the early sixties when it was possible to walk freely into the cultural section of the American Embassy and browse among things American and even borrow records of American music. My first encounter with Charles Ives's music, for example, belongs to that period. Since then, in my teaching of twentieth-century music, I have increasingly felt the need to introduce my students to American music given that the Americanness of American music is modern—it has found its voice during our century. Although it is customary to admire America's vast industrial, architectural and scientific achievements, its rapid development as a musical nation is no less remarkable. The aim of this book is to trace this spectacular development and to draw attention to some of the works of a number of composers who have made an important contribution to the forging of an authentic American musical identity.

The author is fully aware that there are several significant composers missing from these pages who, for one reason or other, could—or perhaps should—have been included. Names which immediately come to mind are Leonard Bernstein, Lucas Foss, William Schuman and the emerging names of such women composers as Alison Knowles, Meredith Monk, Pauline Oliveros and Shulamit Ran. But a canonical approach and the desire to establish some basic facts and characteristic developments meant selectivity. It is proof of the richness of the American musical scene, which abounds in musical talent, that I feel apologetic for not having included more composers. The select bibliography, however, gives the interested reader further material for exploration.

Music as a form of non-verbal communication plays or should play an important role in our emotional and intellectual lives. It has a life-enhancing and enriching effect without which it is quite possible to live, but not as well. Moreover, it has the power to reveal both individual and national characteristics. As a means of human expression it is worthy of our attention if we are to understand and tolerate each other. In order to understand, we must learn to decipher signs—messages, as it were—and to make ourselves aware of what is going on around us. Approaching music by verbal means is likely to be less satisfying, if not frustrating at times, than the real thing, live music. This book aims to be an introductory guide for eventually experiencing real American sound.

Aaron Copland once said, "If a literary man puts together two words about music one of them will be wrong." I agree. Anyone who writes about music, even a musicologist, is forced to verbalise about a non-verbal art. Yet I believe that music is so important that it is worth the risk of putting two words together in the hope that one of them will be right.

Otto Karolyi
University of Stirling

Acknowledgements

I should like to express my warmest thanks and gratitude to the following people who patiently and critically read my manuscript and who spotted and corrected numerous errors: my wife, Benedikte, my son Julian and his wife Emma. Thanks are also due to Bill Macdonald for his encouraging comments, to Elspeth Gillespie for her loyalty and most reliable typing, and finally to Andrew Lindesay of Cygnus Arts who edited this book.

Modern American Music

1
Background, Part 1
A Land without Musical Tradition:
In Search of Roots

What kind of music is most necessary to men—scholarly or folk music?
Leo Tolstoy

IT WAS ALEXIS DE TOCQUEVILLE (1805–1859) WHO observed that, as a nation, America had no infancy. The country seemed to him to have by-passed certain characteristic phases of growth shared by all other nations and emerged fully-fledged out of the wilderness. Apart from its English-speaking settlers, immigrants to America had to give up their languages and more or less everything that mattered culturally. America grew as a nation from the dedicated work of uprooted peoples who, to start with, hardly had time and energy for culture. It is no wonder that de Tocqueville wrote in 1831: "America has hitherto produced very few writers of distinction; it possesses no great historians, and not a single eminent poet. The inhabitants of that country look upon literature properly so-called with a kind of disapprobation . . ."[1] This observation could also have been justifiably applied to music.

By the end of the century the picture had changed quite considerably, but music seemed to lag behind the arts and sciences. The reasons for this are complex. Apart from a lack of tradition in art music, the patchy imports of folk and church music of English, Irish, Scottish and other European origins, together with Negro and Indian traditions, did not integrate with ease. Musical institutions and the idea of proper musical education were slow to emerge and the musical professions were viewed with contempt by the average American. Music was largely left to be performed by invited foreigners in the midst of this evolving nation of foreigners. The emergence of America's musical independence, that is, the creation of a music with a characteristic profile, is thus an entirely twentieth-century phenomenon. Music as a significant art form came into its own in America during the twentieth century, well after her sister disciplines of literature and fine art. But before turning to the discussion of American art music, at least a cursory glance should be given to its musical background, a background that lies in religious music, in diverse folk traditions, including black music, and in the popular/ patriotic songs, among other 'vernacular'[2] musical manifestations and sources.

Psalms and Hymn Singing

It would be a mistake to assume that the passengers of the Mayflower, in which the Pilgrim Fathers voyaged in 1620, brought little culture with them. As far as music is concerned, they took with them the important spiritual and musical heritage of psalm singing as well as their native English folk tradition. This voyage to the 'new found land' took place in the aftermath of the great Elizabethan age which had been one of the most spectacular musical periods in the history of England. The founding fathers and mothers thus contributed a musical legacy which was one of the many significant strands that make up the rich diversity of America's musical tradition. De Tocqueville was not able to take this into consideration—indeed, he ignored music in his assessment of American culture.

One aspect of that legacy was the chanting of psalms in Protestant churches. This followed the old practice of the Catholic church. However, 'psalms' eventually became a loosely-used term for most sung sacred music. The importance attached to psalm singing can best be illustrated by the fact that Henry Ainsworth's *Book of Psalmes: Englished Both in Prose and Metre* (1612), was second only to the Bible of the Pilgrims in importance. During the seventeenth and eighteenth centuries other books came into popular circulation, notably Sternhold and Hopkin's *Whole Book of Psalmes*, referred to as the 'Old Version' (1562), and Thomas Ravenscroft's *Whole Book of Psalmes* (1621). Stylistically, the musical content of these collections reflected their times well and contained, apart from 'Englished' elements, traces of continental folk elements as well. After all, many of the Pilgrims were 'Separatists' and had been exiled for their religious beliefs before their historic journey to America, some having fled already to Holland in 1609. The Franco-Dutch influence on their Psalmody was acknowledged by Ainsworth in his foreword:

> . . . The singing-notes, therefore, I have most taken from our former Englished Psalms, when they will fit the measure of the verse. And for the other long verses I have also taken (for the most part) the gravest and easiest tunes of the French and Dutch Psalms . . .

The Dutch and French settlers carried on their own tradition of singing in their Reformed Church. And sing they did, ardently, and in their own language.

The English for their part published, as early as 1640, what is now known as the *Bay Psalm Book* or *New England Psalm Book*. Its original title was *The Whole Booke of Psalmes Faithfully Translated into English Metre*. It is notable that the first book ever printed in English in the New World was a verbal and, by implication, musical expression of worship. Originally, the congregations followed by ear well-known tunes passed down the generations, such as "O God we with our ears have heard, / Our Fathers have us told . . ." Not until the ninth edition, which appeared in 1698, was the *Bay Psalm Book* enriched by the actual inclusion of music. There were, of course, several later publications, notably, *A New Collection of Psalm Tunes Adaption to Congregational Worship* (1774), but it is sufficient here to draw attention to those few which served as the foundation stones for the musical life of America.

With the increasing need for congregational and choral singing, it was necessary to provide a coherent guide to singing technique as singing by ear was felt to be less than satisfactory. The compilation of a guide for singing was successfully carried out by Rev. John Tufts (1689–1750) in Newbury, Massachusetts. He surfaced at the right time to fulfil a growing demand in the main 'singing-schools' that had sprung up all

over the country. The idea behind the singing-schools was to
channel congregational singing, hitherto based on aural tradition, into 'strict singing' led by trained and expert psalmodists.
This was a move towards making psalm singing, which had
become something of an aurally transmitted folk tradition, into
a more musically literate—and therefore a more professional—
kind of 'regular singing'. Those who believed in the 'good old
way' did not give up easily, as its 'free style' was practised
right up to the end of the nineteenth century. Be that as it may,
Rev. Tufts was among the first who compiled *A Very Plain and
Easy Introduction to the Singing of Psalm Tunes* (1721), which was
to serve the needs of the new singing-schools.

During the eighteenth century, hymn singing gradually
took precedence over psalm singing. As one would expect, this
development was closely related to theological developments
and changes leading to several religious revivals well into our
own century. Suffice it to say, the most influential British contributions and influences in American hymnody were those of
Isaac Watts (1674–1748) whose texts became popular, as did the
hymns of the two Wesleys, John Wesley (1703–1791) and
Charles Wesley (1707–1788), whose two compilations were
entitled *Collection of Psalms and Hymns* (1737) and *Hymns to
Sacred Poems* (1739). It is noteworthy that in the second collection the psalms were omitted and, moreover, when the first
genuine American collection appeared in 1789, its title, *Divine
Hymns or Spiritual Songs*, was to herald a significant genre of
black music.

Folk Music

For reasons which are multifarious, folk music is seldom a
straightforward subject. In the context of America, the problem
is made even more complex by the diversity of the ethnic
groups involved: the clearest characteristic of American folk
music is its many faceted nature. This colourful palette of
sound originates from European, Asian, African and American
Indian sources, all adding their distinct voices, and, indeed
finally losing them to form a voice which became American by

virtue of its stylistic diversity and of its hybrid nature. The strong spiritual need and ability of immigrants to retain some of their national characteristics through music, even if in some modified form, was made clear by Cecil Sharp (1859–1924), in collaboration with Maude Karpeles (1885–1976), in their fascinating collection *English Folk Songs from the Southern Appalachians* (1917–1918), which demonstrated that the English folk tradition was kept alive there while in England it was all but forgotten. Moreover, one of the most characteristic developments to stand out in the history of American music is the cross-fertilisation of Anglo-American and African music.

Afro-American Music

It is worth remembering that from the sixteenth century to the middle of the nineteenth century, that is, to the year of the Proclamation of Emancipation (1863), almost sixteen million Africans were uprooted from their ancestral lands and homes and enslaved. The African slaves brought with them the only things they could: the memories of their customs and the rich tradition of their own indigenous artistic and religious expressions, in which music has always had a major role to play.

It is a characteristic and powerful attribute of music to be able to serve as spiritual solace. And solace was indeed in demand. The African encounter with Christianity via the inhumanity of slavery must have been a bewildering experience. Man failed, but the Christian faith with its message of inherent justice, even if not necessarily on this earth, gave hope and a framework in which to live, even if mostly at survival level. From the amalgamation of the largely Anglo-American Protestant faith with the American tradition of the slaves, a style of worship and communal music emerged, which now is generally acknowledged to contain significant African origins. By the nineteenth century, the Afro-American style of music-making was a well-established practice.

In the religious context it meant adapting hymn and psalm singing to a highly individual Afro-American genre of sung spirituals. The individuality of this genre is characterised by improvised singing where the structure of alternating line and refrain of the texts invite the singers to perform in an exotic, if not ecstatic, style marked by strong rhythms. The mood is usually sad, verging on a lament in which the singers identify with the suffering and death of Christ, but with unfailing hope in God. Such spirituals as 'Nobody knows the trouble I seen', 'Steal away', 'Were you there when they crucified my Lord?', 'Children, we shall be free', and many others have become part of a musical heritage shared by most of us far beyond the shores of America. It is a splendid irony, and a rare example of justice given to the human spirit, that nowadays most people are likely to associate authentic American folk music in one way or other with music created by the African slaves. In this respect they were better vindicated than the unfortunate American Indians.

Popular Songs

Popular music is a genre quite different from folk music, though it can be related to it in several ways. For example, popular music tends to be urban in origin, thus reflecting the values of burghers and industrial workers rather than rural values. An equally important factor is that whereas folk music was the instinctive and orally transmitted creation of a rural and largely illiterate community, the popular song was more likely to be composed by a professional musician and popularised through print. By the late eighteenth and early nineteenth centuries the most popular entertainments were the ballad operas which were packed with catchy tunes and rough comic scenes. *The Beggar's Opera* (1728), with text by John Gay (1685–1732) and music by Johann Christoph Pepusch (1667–1752), was performed as early as 1750 in New York. The ballad operas and comic operettas also introduced the singing black man, mostly in a comic context, and so launching minstrel shows, with their impersonations of black people by white singers, achieving a long-lasting popularity.

During the nineteenth century, there was also a vogue for Irish and Scottish tunes, ensuring the popularity of songs like 'The Last Rose of Summer', 'Minstrel Boy' and 'The Blue Bells of Scotland' among dozens of others. Some were of folk origin but were revamped, as it were, with up-to-date accompaniments and often with new texts.

Among several distinguished popular song-writers of the nineteenth century who emerged in America, the name of Stephen Foster (1826–1864) stands out with the folk-like, natural simplicity of his melodic writing. He had a gift for largely melancholic but catchy texts and tunes such as 'Oh! Susanna', 'Old Folks at Home', 'My old Kentucky home, good night!', his output totalling two hundred in all. His success, in terms of sold copies, was quite spectacular. It enabled this talented musician of Irish origin to devote his energies to popular song-writing full-time—a rare thing in his time and country.

Patriotic music also belongs to the popular music industry. All nations indulge in this brand of music-making and the Americans too have created a corpus of patriotic songs, especially during the time of the Civil War. Such popular titles as 'The Bonnie Blue Flat', 'The Drummer Boy of Shiloh', 'When Johnny comes marching home', speak for themselves. Such patriotic songs often used traditional tunes of English, Irish and Scottish origin, but with new texts reflecting contemporary events.

Art Music with Foreign Models

The music of America, before it found its own voice, was also indebted to some composers whose contributions, during most of the nineteenth century, paved the way for the creation of art or concert music. Without this, one can only talk of musical culture in anthropological and ethno-musicological terms. The musical style of the nineteenth century was largely dominated by Austro-German masters both in Europe and in America. Most nineteenth-century American composers not only studied in Germany but also based their own compositions on

Austro/German models. Thus William Mason (1829–1908), a pianist and pedagogue who largely composed for the piano, followed the styles of Brahms, Chopin and Liszt. James Parker (1828–1916), a dedicated sacred music composer was influenced by the work of Mendelssohn. John Pain (1839–1906) took Beethoven as his model for his symphonies and choral works, especially Symphony No.1 and the Mass in D. Several other prestigious names, including George Chadwick (1854–1931), made some ingenious efforts to integrate aspects of indigenous American music, notably the Afro-American song style, within the Teutonic musical framework.

Taking models in art is a perfectly legitimate, indeed necessary practice. It is not satisfactory, however, when the user of a model is not able to transcend and metamorphose into his own language what has been learned from that model. The overall result is then epigonistic—that is, imitative. In England, Edward Elgar, whose life covers roughly the same period as those listed above, provides a relevant contrast. He too largely modelled his music on the same Austrian and German composers as some of his American counterparts, but his genius, as his best works show, succeeded in transcending the influences of the models and in becoming a new as well as individual English voice. The same cannot be said for his American counterparts, but they represent a bridge between the European classical music heritage which they imported and practised in their own country and the tentative beginnings of American art music which they pioneered with dedication.

This brief survey of American music from the early sixteenth to the end of the nineteenth centuries, forming the first of the two chapters devoted to background information, can only touch upon some of the ways in which American music evolved. It is a complex and fascinating story, as well as being a moving example of man's struggle for expression and identity. Armed with this basic knowledge, and having paid due attention to it, we can now turn to the discussion of one of the first twentieth-century composers to succeed in forging an autonomous American musical style.

2
Businessman and Musical Genius: Charles Ives

This fascinating composer . . . was exploring the 1960s during
the heyday of Strauss and Debussy.
Igor Stravinsky

EVEN TODAY, CHARLES IVES IS OFTEN SEEN AS A 'primitive' like the French painter Rousseau and as a musical equivalent of the American painter Grant Wood (1892–1942) and perhaps the novelist Thomas Wolfe (1900–1938). But these comparisons throw only a partial light on Ives's music. He was a complex character with immense abilities in the fields of both business and music. This dual or, indeed, ambivalent gift, caused at least one of his critics and fellow composers Virgil Thomson to believe that Ives did not have the courage to commit himself fully to his art: " . . . For it is not teaching that cripples; no master has ever feared that. It is gentility; not giving one's all to art".[1] This somewhat lofty view aside, the genteel Ives did more for his art and country than many a so-called fully-committed artist whose work, it turns out, so often disappears without trace.

Ives was born into a musical family in 1874. His father was a band-master and his mother a singer of some distinction. His musical education was eccentric, but thorough, and strongly flavoured with American Transcendentalism. The family took pride in the fact that they had once entertained Ralph Waldo Emerson (1803–1882) when he gave lectures in Danbury, Connecticut in 1859. The Transcendentalist world view, with its emphasis on intuition and the importance of the individual conscience, helped form Ives and stayed with him for the rest of his life. The most important formative influence was, however, his congenial father, George Ives (1845–1894). His impact can hardly be exaggerated—he was his main teacher and an

enlightened, playful and understanding friend to whom
Charles could turn for advice and encouragement until the
major blow of his untimely death. Ives then lost a like-minded
fellow musician with whom he could freely share his ideas and
musical experiments. After his father's death, he studied at
Yale University under Horatio Parker (1863–1919), graduating
in 1898. He kept his activities as a composer to himself, both at
home in Danbury and when he was a student at Yale. Although
he could have followed his father's footsteps by becoming a
professional organist and composer, Ives decided against it
and instead of living as a struggling artist, he chose insurance
as a career. Working mostly in New York, he eventually
founded, with his partner Julian Myrich, his own firm and
together they ran it with exemplary efficiency.

Ives prospered and in 1930 was able to retire from his company while still in his mid-fifties. His attitude to insurance was
philanthropic—he believed that insurance cover should be
made available to all income groups. The Mutual Life Insurance Company had a visionary executive in Ives, whose application of Transcendentalist attitudes was as good for business
as it was for his clients. In order to train his insurance agents,
Ives wrote a handbook called *The Amount to Carry—Measuring
the Prospect*, which remained in use for many decades and is
regarded as a classic of its kind. Its content shows Ives's ideal-
istic stand and his firm belief in progress, reason and the
enrichment of life. To these ends, he declared, the insurance
company was doing its part.

If we also consider his innovation of what is known as
'estate planning', which became an everyday concept among
life insurance men, it is clear that Ives was highly inventive
and original in the field of business. There he functioned successfully with no sign of conflict regarding his art. Yet there is
something strange in the image of the responsible and well-to-
do businessman on the one hand and, on the other, the private
world of the experimental composer who, during evenings,
weekends and holidays, composed with relentless fervour,
throwing used sheets of manuscript paper behind his back
onto the floor, where they remained unorganised. But on these

scattered sketches, the first authentically American art music was written. Ives was isolated from most of the European developments which were taking place during the first quarter of the twentieth century, but he nevertheless created a substantial body of works that paralleled, and even anticipated with his singular originality, compositional innovations which are now largely attributed to Europe. His fame as a composer rests on a prodigious quantity of compositions which he created from the time of his first *Psalm Settings* (1894) to about the end of the First World War.

What is striking about Ives's music is its tunefulness. But, and here one must tread cautiously, apart from his own material, which could be as popular in flavour as the best of Stephen Foster's songs, he made liberal use of borrowed material, whether hymn tunes, folk-songs, popular tunes, or Beethoven, with an absolute confidence in his ability to transform these into his own distinctive sound. A sense of fun pervades many of his scores, but, above all, there is a desire to communicate his musical 'idea', and to ensure that everybody experiences it. His music incorporates the trivial and banal as well as the elevated and spiritual. There is a similarity between his enthusiastic vision of wanting to spread the benefits of life insurance and his desire to make music accessible to as many people as possible. He believed that business and music helped each other in experiencing the 'fullness of life'. He was a highly sophisticated populist who, preferring privacy, shied away from publicity.

Another of Ives's traits was his ability to discard traditional thinking when he felt it necessary. This was done not with the rebellious mind of the revolutionary, but with an inner sense of freedom—he was not looking over his shoulder for approval. That is why he is mistakenly thought of as 'naïve' or 'primitive'. On the contrary, his music could be called 'atraditional'—that is, irreverent, free-spirited and, indeed, American. Already in his youth, he experimented with writing a set of fugues which were in four simultaneously played keys. These student efforts found a more definite form in his *Fugue in Four Keys*, or the *Shining Shore* (1897). This was an introductory essay in polytonality which was later to become an increasingly used procedure in modern music. Another early tongue-in-cheek composition was his *Variation on 'America'* (1891)—the theme of which is better known in Britain as 'God Save the Queen'. This, piece of youthful exuberance, full of Ives's humour, is nowadays mostly performed in its orchestral version of the 1960s scored by William Schuman (b. 1910).

Central Park in the Dark (1906) is less a Debussy-like nocturne and more a spirited mimicry of nocturnal sound effects in an urban environment, especially in its central section, where the cacophonous climax includes the distant sounds of a bar-piano. The orchestration is superbly evocative and, with its mysterious string sections, the work enters the realm of expressionism. This piece is all the more remarkable because Ives knew nothing of expressionism and its European exponents, Schoenberg, Berg and Webern. In *The Unanswered Question* (1908), Ives surprises us with an unusual combination of instruments by writing for four flutes (or two flutes, oboe and clarinet), a trumpet and, playing off-stage, a muted string ensemble (this can be a quartet or string orchestra). The three groups of instrumentalists have a symbolic role to play in the form of silence and dialogue, the strings representing audible silence, the trumpet, existential questioning, and the flutes, the unsuccessful responses. The separation of the strings creates a kind of stereophonic effect in this strange composition whose subtitle was originally 'A Cosmic Landscape'. As the increasing speeds attempt to answer the slow questioning of the trumpet, not only is a poly-rhythmic texture created but there is also an element of chance in the music. It is no exaggeration to say that in this piece as well as in others, he had anticipated ideas which were later to be explored by Edgard Varèse and John Cage.

Perhaps his most popular composition is what is now known as *Three Places in New England* (1903–1914), formerly called *First Orchestral Set* or *A New England Symphony*. This is clearly a programmatic work in three movements, although each movement is a self-contained symphonic poem with a descriptive heading. The heading for the first movement, 'Boston Common' (1911), is in the form of a poem which is likely to have been written by the composer himself:

'The monument to Colonel Shaw and his colored regiment
by St Gaudens'

Moving—Marching—Faces of Souls!
Marked with generations of pain,
Part-free of a Destiny,
Slow, restlessly—swaying us on with you
Towards other Freedom.
The man on horseback, carved from
A native quarry of the World Liberty
And from what your country was made.
You images of a Divine Law
Carved in the shadow of a saddened heart—
Never light abandoned—
Of an age and of a nation.
Above and beyond that compelling mass
Rises a drum-beat of the common-heart
In the silence of a strange and
Sounding afterglow
Moving—Marching—Faces of Souls!

With this Whitmanesque invocation, Ives evokes mysterious marches and tunes of distant times.

The second movement has the following heading:

'No. 2. Putnam's Camp, Redding, Connecticut (1912)'

Near Redding Center, Conn., is a small park preserved as a Revolutionary Memorial; for here General Israel Putnam's soldiers had their winter quarters in 1778–1778. Long rows of stone camp fireplaces still remain to stir a child's imagination. The hardship which the soldiers endured and the agitation of a few hot-heads to break camp and march onto the Hartford Assembly for relief, is part of Redding history . . .

He goes on to describe a child who, while dreaming when on a picnic organised by the First Church and the Village Cornet Band, encounters a woman who reminds him of the Goddess of Liberty and he hears the soldiers marching "with fife and drum". When the great General Putnam turns up to the cheers of his soldiers, the little boy wakes up and "runs down past the monument to listen to the band" with his friends.

For this second movement, Ives resurrected two of his earlier compositions, the *Overture 1776* and *Country Band March*, both from 1903, and incorporated them into a homogeneous whole together with several well-known tunes such as 'The British Grenadiers', 'Arkansas Traveller' and 'Marching Through Georgia'. Not unlike Mahler, Ives was struck by the way events can occur simultaneously in life—joy and sorrow, the sound of the hurdy-gurdy, the marching soldiers' song, or indeed, two or more bands playing different tunes at the same time in complete disregard of each other. Mahler craftily amalgamated these impressions into the Austro-German symphonic Lieder structure. Ives, on the other hand, retained much of their realistic effect. His music is often not so much polyphonic, in the traditional sense, but multi-layered in his very individual style. *Three Places in New England* as a whole, and its second movement in particular, is a masterly demonstration of Ives's musical thought anticipating compositional practice as far ahead as Lucio Berio.

The third movement, 'The Housatonic at Stockbridge (1914)' was inspired by a poem by Robert Underwood Johnson, 'Contented river! in thy dreamy realm'. The third movement of this remarkable set of symphonic poems was apparently also inspired by a memorable Sunday morning walk with his young wife. Thus the veiled hymn tune, as if heard from a distance through the slowly lifting morning mists at the river, has a personal dimension also. These three movements do not hold together as a tightly fitting symphonic whole, although the first and third movements show some relationship, though this may be incidental. They are, however, highly original compositions in which personal and national elements achieve an authentic expression which is American to the core.

Even Ives's symphonies were not always conceived as unified wholes but were gathered together from diverse sources and material written at different times, as is the case with his Holiday Symphony. A tendency towards fragmentation and additive compositional technique is an aspect of his work which one must come to terms with when listening to his music.

He wrote five symphonies in all (or six if one includes *Three Places in New England*). Symphony no. 1 in D minor (1896–1898) was written while he was still studying at Yale under Horatio Parker and is a graduation work in which he tried faithfully to emulate the European symphonic style. Nevertheless, to the great alarm of his master, he already showed a tendency to treat tonality rather freely, undermining the key of D minor by writing a subject which modulated to numerous keys. Symphony no. 2 (1901) is a mellow mélange of genuine American popular tunes. Here, Ives captured the atmosphere of the Connecticut countryside which he skilfully evoked in liberal quotations of folk tunes, popular tunes, hymns and dance music in a celebration of his beloved country, one of the songs quoted being 'America the Beautiful'.

In 1904 Ives completed his Symphony no. 3. His inspiration is again deeply rooted in the American past, notably in the once popular camp meetings in Danbury. The mood is largely religious, perhaps because both the first and third movements were originally for organ, but also because of Ives's own nostalgic evocations of worship. The quotations are largely old American hymn tunes such as 'O for a Thousand Tongues' and 'Just as I am'. The composer added a heading to this symphony, 'The Camp Meeting', and the three movements are titled 'Old Folks' Gatherin'', 'Children's Day' and 'Communion' respectively.

In Ives's Symphony no. 4 (1910–1916), the fundamental questions 'what?' and 'why?' are asked. The answers are given in the three movements which follow the first short prelude movement. Scored for a vast orchestra, this symphony is also based on adaptation of earlier materials and its final completion took some sorting out well after the death of the composer. Leopold Stokowski, who gave its world première in 1965, thought it one of the most demanding compositions he had ever conducted. In one section, for example, there is an assortment of twenty-seven rhythmic patterns played at the same time. In this work too, Ives introduces and superimposes an array of familiar melodies from 'Marching Through Georgia' to Handel's 'Joy to the World'. The poly-grouping of instrumental ensembles is also apparent, especially in the finale where three instrumental groups appear in the order of percussion, main orchestra and a chamber ensemble of five violins and harp. And, in addition to all this, there is a choir to lend extra colour. The total effect of this sometimes overwhelming work operates on two levels. On one level, the listener hears great symphonic music of exhilarating and strange beauty, while on another, one is confronted with a collage of American musical history through a myriad of melodic references from the Pilgrim Fathers to barn-dance music. In Ives's music one is perpetually made aware of the rich heritage of sacred and secular popular American music which he transplanted into the realm of art music, without caring much about metamorphosing them as had been the case with every other art music composer including Mozart, Beethoven and Schubert. Ives leaves the vernacular tunes to express their own integrity and by doing so he offers us at once the sophisticated and the popular. He is among the few modern composers whose modernism—embracing polytonality, polyrhythm, collage, cacophony and so on—is engaging and palatable because of its immediacy. A playfulness permeates even his most difficult and mysterious evocations.

His four-movement *A Symphony: Holidays* (1913) was, yet again, assembled from materials which he had composed at different periods, the last movement dating, for example, from as early as 1904. The composer himself suggested that the movements could be played as separate symphonic movements, or just "lumped together as a symphony". Like *Three Places in New England*, *Holidays* is also programmatic. The composer indicated on the score that the whole work was something of a "Recollection of a boy's holidays in a Connecticut country town". The headings to each movement are 'Washington's Birthday', 'Decoration Day', 'Fourth of July' and, lastly, 'Thanksgiving' (or 'Forefathers'). It is immediately apparent that Ives was aiming to evoke, by purely musical means, an American life and history through a child's remembrances, of "boyish mischief", of the joy of hearing band music at national holidays and of the revered Puritan forefathers. It is no wonder that he liked the composition, especially the third movement, of which he commented "My God, that's the best thing I've done yet".

The *Universe Symphony* (1911–1951) only exists as a general outline yet it reveals Ives's lifelong preoccupation with Transcendentalist thought in general and his interest in giving musical expression to abstract ideas in particular. The vast scope of his unfulfilled intentions can be seen by the three programmatic titles which he jotted down—'Past: Formation of the waters and mountains', 'Present: Earth, evolution in nature and humanity' and 'Future: Heaven, the rise of all to the Spiritual'. Ives was contemplating a project which to an extent paralleled the work of the Russian composer Scriabin (1872–1915) who also set out to write compositions on a grand scale involving all the senses and culminating in ecstasy. Both composers were seeking after the spiritual in music and the powerful mystery of art. Here the similarities end, as Ives did not share Scriabin's obsessive and self-indulgent mysticism based on a late romantic compound of the demonic and the erotic. When Ives refers to spiritual values, he is in earnest, unlike his Russian contemporary, who had a tendency, like so many of his compatriots, towards a messianic voluptuousness. Nothing was further from Ives's way of thinking. *The Universe Symphony* remained an unrealised idea but is nevertheless of interest.

Ives's chamber music output is no less impressive, comprising four violin sonatas and two string quartets as well as several compositions for the keyboard. Of the two outstanding piano sonatas, the Piano Sonata no. 2 (*Concord, Mass., 1840–1860*) of 1911–1915, usually referred to as the *Concord* Sonata, is his better known major contribution to the genre. Again, the programmatic content is made self-evident by titles given to each of the four movements: 'Emerson', 'Hawthorne', 'The Alcotts' and 'Thoreau'. This work is something of an apotheosis of Ives's profound belief in and, indeed, his ultimate homage to and affirmation of Transcendentalism. It is a musical celebration of his beloved New England and its literary life in the mid-nineteenth century. The names given to each movement are those who influenced him most in his thinking. Emerson had been admired by his parents and it was impossible for Ives not to react to the teaching of the endearing and self-made Branson Alcott (1799–1888), who advocated the importance of schooling children in leisurely conditions with ennobling music and Socratic dialogues. The central idea of the Transcendentalist was that, in a world in which all seems to conspire against the individual, the truly free man must, by the very nature of things, be a non-conformist. It was an idea founded on self-realisation and self-reliance and one that made a deep impression on Ives. Indeed, it would not be far-fetched to propose that Ives's music is a continuation, if not a realisation in sound, of what the transcendentalists were advocating in literature before him.

In the *Concord* Sonata, Ives also incorporated, and not for the first time, his favourite musical motif, the famous four notes which open Beethoven's Symphony no. 5. Ives believed that certain musical utterances, such as this, had an archetypal and universal meaning. If this were so, he saw no reason why archetypal musical ideas should not be re-employed, further developed and commented upon by other composers of subsequent generations. The work is difficult and contains technical tricks with overtones, the use of a wooden plank to hold down notes over two octaves which introduced the idea of sound-clusters, as well as other harmonic and rhythmic complexities. In the last movement, 'Thoreau', even a flute is called for to add a spiritual dimension. Wilfrid Mellers, in his book *Music in a New Found Land*, shrewdly asked "The 'flute' melody is in or around Bb (is it an accident that this was the Alcott's key, representatives of the 'common heart' of *Concord*?)".[2]

Another of Ives's stylistic and perhaps philosophical hallmarks is his tendency to let his compositions fade away at the end, as if abandoning them or allowing the music to disintegrate. This is very marked in the *Concord* Sonata where the opening movement 'Emerson' ends in this style, and the final bar of the whole sonata is deliberately left inconclusive by combining the tonic and the dominant chords to create an unresolved tonic seventh in D minor which vibrates in a mysterious and questioning way. (Ravel's use of the same chord at the end of *L'Enfant et les Sortilèges* (1920–1925), because of its strong dominant-thirteenth move to the tonic-seventh, creates a halo of enchantment over the second syllable of the word "Maman" which ends this remarkable opera.) Ives's spacing of the tonic seventh chord on the other hand gives greater prominence to the dominant, thus emphasising the duality of this chord, resulting in an impression of incompleteness, as if there were more to come. R. S. Perry, in her book, *Charles Ives and the American Mind*, offers an interesting reading of this characteristic: "Probability and human nature often leave problems unsolved, so Ives's endings are often confessions of the irresolvable complexities of life".[3]

The *Concord* Sonata stands as a towering accomplishment comparable in stature to Liszt's Piano Sonata in B Minor. The importance given to this work by the composer himself is indicated by the fact that he not only published it at his own expense but also felt the need to write *Essays Before a Sonata* (1920), in order to explain his intentions. He even felt defensive enough to give this collection of essays an ironic dedication to those unable to understand either his music or his essays.

Ives was also a most prolific song writer with over 150 songs to his credit. Stylistically they cover a range from the simplest cowboy songs to the most daringly modern art songs, such as 'Paracelsus' (1921) based on Browning's poem of the same title. As was the case with his *Concord* Sonata, Ives financed the publication in 1922 of *114 Songs*, comprising a large selection of his songs dating from 1884. The collection is ordered in a typical Ivesian topsy-turvy way. The collection starts with a song he wrote in 1921, 'Majority', based on his own text, and is numbered in reverse order back to the song of his youth, 'Slow March' (1884). This arrangement makes sense—indeed, it was Bertrand Russell who suggested that, for a better understanding not only of the past but of the present, history should be studied in reverse chronology by starting today and working backwards. In the first song 'Majority', extreme harmonic progressions are used together with toneclusters. Looking at this and other scores of Ives, the impression is that many modernists were rather conservative in comparison. In *114 Songs* one can see the exuberant originality, the free nature of the songs' creativeness, and, above all, their Americanness.

The First World War, the collapse of the Wilsonian dream of peace and the recognition of the hopelessness of the noble dream of the League of Nations, all aggravated the increasing heart trouble from which Ives had been suffering for years. In the early 1920s, he began to compose less and from 1926 onwards he practically abandoned composing altogether. He retired completely from business in 1930 as a recluse at his farm in Connecticut until his death in 1954.

With Thomas Edison, or more recently, the physicist and Nobel Laureate Feynman, Ives shared a free pioneering spirit and inventiveness. During his creative period, he poured out new ideas and in so doing, he anticipated many musical ideas well before his time. But his greatest achievement was to have forged a truly authentic American art music.

3
Background, Part 2
Popular Music as a National Style:
Gospel Song, Blues, Ragtime, Jazz
and Tin Pan Alley

*The future music of this country must be founded on
what are called the Negro melodies.*
Antonin Dvořák

OUT OF THE RICH TAPESTRY OF BOTH SACRED
and secular vernacular music of the American past
there evolved a series of distinct musical styles, which,
for the sake of convenience, will be considered here under the
much used though ill-defined title of popular music.[1] This is
nevertheless a genre and one which not only became the pre-
dominant musical expression of America but also influenced
musical expression around the world. It is hardly possible to
discuss American art music without referring, at least in passing, to the influence of the blues and jazz and their related
forms. The most successful representatives of American music,
with a world-wide appeal, were its popular musicians, and
these were predominantly black Americans. In general, one
could say that whereas relatively few people have heard of
Ives, Cowell or Ruggles, hardly anyone would claim ignorance
of Louis Armstrong or Duke Ellington. One could hardly label
the spiritual or Gospel songs 'light' music, though they were
certainly popular. Yet they are a folk and popular form of
musical expression with a particularly 'jazzy' style of interpretation and for this reason it is fitting to discuss them under this
heading. The spiritual, to which Gospel song is related, has
already been discussed in Chapter 1.

Gospel Song

Theologically, the Gospel hymnology belongs to the Protestant evangelical gatherings of the mid-nineteenth century of both black and white denominations. As so often happens, the living practice was followed up by the publication of song books, notably *Gospel Songs* (1874) by P. P. Bliss and *Gospel Hymns and Sacred Songs* (1875) by P. P. Bliss and Ira D. Sankey. The term 'Gospel song' was introduced in these books.

Although Gospel music is largely a nineteenth- and twentieth-century development, the Gospel song comes from a long tradition of spiritual and hymn singing, the origin of its form going back to the singing style of white preachers in the sixteenth and seventeenth centuries. At that time, the church leader would intone some article of faith which would then be repeated by the congregation. During the mid-nineteenth century, Sunday schools relied heavily on Gospel singing, as it was recognised as a useful means of propagating the Gospel, and during the second half of the nineteenth century after the Civil War, the growing influence of the white fundamentalist revival made itself felt. One of the most interesting features which emerged during this post-Civil War period was the cross fertilisation of sacred and secular tunes. Hymns and other sacred songs including Gospel songs, were influenced by marches and popular parlour and theatre songs, with both music and texts often sentimental. In general, the texts of Gospel songs are subjective and comforting, their range of tone extending from devotion to militant evangelism. But the most striking contribution was that of the Afro-American 'call and response', or leader and chorus, mainly taken from their work songs. The 'response' was often improvised by a group of singers, for example a vocal quartet or a choir, and incorporated an instinctive use of syncopation and 'blue notes' for good measure. An amalgamation from these diverse sources made the singing of both spirituals and Gospel songs a profoundly felt Afro-American, and to a lesser extent white American, religious expression. As Gospel singing is closely related to the spiritual, the distinction between them is often blurred. The types of spirituals, such as 'Camp-meeting' spirituals, 'sorrow-songs' and 'jubilee spirituals' are intermingled with white Gospel music. Well-known examples of Gospel songs include 'Come unto me and rest!', 'Brighten the corner where you are!', 'Go down Moses', 'Steal Away', 'Swing Low Sweet Chariot', 'Something within me' and 'I shall wear a crown'. Both genres are striking examples of a mélange of white and black styles of communal musical expression, bound together by the vigorous Protestant evangelical faith which they reflect in an ecstatic, subjectively direct and personal manner.

From the 1930s onwards, spiritual and Gospel singing entered the concert halls and their popularity increased with the help of recording. Whenever and wherever they are performed, they not only remind one of misery and suffering, but also of faith, hope and the strength of the human spirit. It was with the help of music that the uprooted and brutally dispersed black people maintained unity and sustained hope.

Blues

It could be argued that the blues, although vaguely related to or at least cross-fertilised with jazz, are more likely than the spiritual to be a form of Afro-American folk-music. Blues echoes its origin in black work-songs and is closely linked to the spiritual and to Gospel songs, but whereas in the spiritual, personal and collective chagrin is channelled towards God, in the blues the singer emphatically expresses his own disappointments or hopes. The frequent references to alcohol, gambling, prostitution and sex, sometimes bluntly expressed, indicate moreover, their urban origins. Spirituals are mostly sung by a group of singers, and, before the 1920s, largely without accompaniment, while the blues singer, on the other hand, is a solo performer with instrumental accompaniment. Similarities between the two genres are to be found in rhythm, especially in the use of syncopation and in the characteristic use of the so-called 'blue notes'. The word 'blue' is a descriptive reference to depression or a melancholic disposition which the blues singer is trying to purge through performance. The lamenting, declamatory style is emphasised by flattening certain notes, the 'blue notes', such as the third and seventh, in a basic twelve bar composition written in a diatonic major scale. As the singer would have it: "The blues ain't nothing' but a good man feelin' bad."

There are various types of blues, as for example, the slow New Orleans and St Louis blues, which are perhaps more popular than the fast Texan variety. It is fair to say that from the 'St Louis Blues' (1914) of W. C. Handy, from Mamie Smith's 'Crazy Blues' (1920) and the immortal performances of blues by Ma Rainey (1886–1939), Bessie Smith (1894–1937) and Billie Holliday (1915–1959), to the campus performers of the 1970s, the blues style made a strong popular impact not only artistically but also as a cultural or social focal point, bringing together aficionados from all races and walks of life.

Ragtime

Ragtime gained popularity during the years 1896–1918 and reached its peak of notoriety around 1910–1915. Its main characteristic of being 'ragged' is through its syncopated rhythm. The first published reference to rag-music dates back to 1896 in the description of a song accompaniment by Ernest Hogan, 'All coons look alike to me'. This was soon followed by numerous publications of rag-music, notably Tom Turpin's (1873–1922) *Harlem Rag* (1897) and *The Ragtime Instructor* by its pianist-composer Ben Harvey (1870–1935) also in 1897. A significant contributing factor to its popularity was its easy availability in print. Light music printing at this time was growing into a big business. Scott Joplin (1868–1917), for example, was one of the greatest exponents of ragtime and sold a million copies of his 'Maple Leaf Rag'. Ragtime was predominantly piano music and as such it has influenced jazz and even left its mark on European composers. As early as 1908, Debussy, influenced by 'Ragtime cake walk',[2] wrote his tongue-in-cheek 'Golliwog's Cake-walk' using the Tristan motif. Stravinsky used ragtime music in *The Soldier's Tale* (1918), in *Ragtime for 11 Instruments* (1918) and in *Piano Rag-music* (1919). In America, Ives himself caught the infectious style and wrote *Ragtime Dances 1–4* (1902–1904) for small orchestra and, again using rag music, First Piano Sonata (1901–1909).

After the First World War, the popularity of ragtime music gave way to jazz. Nowadays there is a renewed interest in ragtime and in some of its principle exponents, such as Tom Turpin and Scott Joplin.

Jazz

The origin of the word 'jazz' has never been satisfactorily traced. In slang it indicates 'putting liveliness or vigour into something' and has acquired sexual connotations. Whatever the etymology may be, as a musical expression it came about at the turn of the century and during the period of the First World War, it established itself firmly. Jazz has multifarious origins and is often assessed as a hybrid form of light music. It is a synthesis of largely Afro-American idioms, principally, Afro-Caribbean rhythm but also spiritual, Gospel and blues performing styles, minstrel music, ragtime and basic European harmony. At the beginning, blues and ragtime playing were hardly distinguishable from jazz but then rag players drifted into jazz. Jazz rapidly took over the scene and by the 1920s the jazz craze was in full swing both in America and in Europe. Buddy Bolden (1878–1931) was among the first important figures to play jazz in his native New Orleans. He played his strange, intoxicating music on the streets as well as in bordellos, referred to as 'pleasure houses'. Storeyville, the red-light district of New Orleans, was the chief employer of the early jazz musicians—an association which to a certain extent still applies today. In jazz gatherings there was an atmosphere not unlike a religious sect meeting with all its ritual, symbols and traditions known only to the participants. The bordellos, night clubs and dance-halls became the churches and chapels of those millions who had been converted to the highly erotic and intoxicating musical ritual of jazz.

New Orleans was the birthplace of the Dixieland Jazz Band in about 1912 and in fact the town gave the world a whole series of fine jazz musicians, the most renowned perhaps being Louis Armstrong (1900–1971). New Orleans was, of course, not alone in developing jazz, as Chicago, New York and many more cities more or less simultaneously started to cultivate and develop their own jazz styles. The 'Jazz Age' was truly launched.

Tin Pan Alley

During the last quarter of the nineteenth century, popular music and especially vocal music, was recognised to be good business. Publishers with foresight and energy made sure of their success by researching the new market to find out what sold well. Most of the leading publishers established their offices on West 28th Street in New York and the nickname given to that street, 'Tin Pan Alley', stuck to both publishers and musicians alike. It was also used to refer to the song-writers (also called 'song-pluggers'—those who performed songs on honky-tonk pianos in their desperate attempt to find fame and money. It was a highly professional and competitive world. Many lost souls as well as outstanding song-writers have walked on the pavements of Tin Pan Alley. The list includes Paul Dresser (1858–1906), Charles Harris (1865–1930), Irving Berlin (1888–1983), Jerome Kern (1885–1943), Cole Porter (1893–1964), Richard Rogers (1902–1980) and many more. One of the most endearing figures of American music, who too was associated with Tin Pan Alley, was George Gershwin and it is to a discussion of his music that we now turn.

4
An American in New York:
George Gershwin

Jazz I regard as an American folk music; not the only one, but a very
powerful one which is probably in the blood and feeling of the American
people more than any other style of folk music.
George Gershwin

EORGE GERSHWIN'S PARENTS WERE EMIGRES
from Russia who met in New York and married there in
1895. In common with many European immigrants at
that time, the authorities, not able to make sense of the foreign
names, changed his father's original surname from Gershovitz
to Gershwin.

George was born in 1898 in New York where he spent the
best part of his life. Musically his parents were of little help as
they had no interest in the arts. Unlike most musicians who
show their talents at an early age, Gershwin could not have
cared less about music for the first dozen or so years of his life.
He was an ordinary boy, good at games but little else. Two
events, however, changed the hitherto sport-orientated boy's
interests—hearing a school mate playing violin while he was
kicking a ball in the yard, and the purchase of a piano for his
brother Ira by his parents in 1910. But it was George, who with
an obsessive zeal, took over the piano. He was lucky to become
a pupil of an imaginative music teacher, Charles Hambitzer,
who had sensed his pupil's great talents. He introduced
Gershwin to some romantic and modern composers' music,
notably Liszt and Debussy. Gershwin's interest, however, was
more towards jazz and popular songs. Having acquired sufficient piano playing skills by the age of sixteen, he left school to
join the profession of the 'song-pluggers' in Tin Pan Alley. It
was there that he started composing, though his ambition was
to work for the theatres on Broadway. Consequently he moved

out of the song publishing and song-pluggers' circles and became a Broadway rehearsal pianist and composer. Soon he was in demand for both his skills.

His first Broadway show, a musical-comedy, *La, La, Lucille* (1919), gave him some notice, and was performed over a hundred times. Then his song 'Nobody But You' became a hit, albeit a modest one in comparison to his smash hit 'Swanee' of the same year. It brought him much attention as well as a substantial royalty of $10,000 in a year. By 1924 he had written several songs and worked for such shows as *Sweet Little Devil* (1924) and even ventured onto the London musical stage with *The Rainbow* (1923) and *Primrose* (1924). His brother, Ira, who turned out to be a gifted writer of lyrics, supplied the text for George's *Lady, Be Good!* (1924). The songs in this show, such as 'Fascinating Rhythm', 'Oh, Lady Be Good!' are now regarded as classics not only in the popular music repertoire but also in concert halls.

It was in the withdrawn work *Blue Monday* (1922), which lasted only one night, that he made his first operatic attempt in Afro-American style and it laid the foundation for an event which launched him to world fame. Paul Whiteman (1890—1967) who was the conductor of the short-lived operatic essay, thought highly of its composer and when he was planning a grandiose concert under the title 'An Experiment in Modern Music', in an attempt to promote jazz and legitimise it in the concert hall, Whiteman commissioned Gershwin to write a composition of symphonic proportions. The place chosen for this memorable concert was New York's Aeolian Hall. There, Gershwin's *Rhapsody in Blue* (1924), was given its first performance there with the composer himself playing the piano. The programme to which Gershwin contributed was an over-ambitious marathon of twenty-six items, which included Elgar's 'Pomp and Circumstance' March no. 1. *Rhapsody in Blue* was a triumph and all the more so as the work was written in a last-minute rush with the help of Ferde Grofe for the orchestration. On the night, Gershwin even improvised some sections.

The music telescopes a youthful rhapsodic temperament, the music of Broadway, Afro-American blues and jazz as well as what Gershwin had learned from his classical music studies, in this instance Liszt. All these ingredients were made to work by Gershwin's vigour and élan. With one inspired master-stroke he succeeded in bringing American popular music to the concert hall. The phenomenal success of *Rhapsody in Blue* made Gershwin a household name and American music acquired a new voice to be reckoned with.

Gershwin's success quickly brought him fame and wealth. A warm-hearted man and a generous entertainer of his friends, he was a charismatic figure, who nevertheless continued to work with relentless energy. He even added painting to his skills and developed a taste for collecting works by modern masters including Modigliani and Picasso. Like Schubert, he too found time to take further tuition to increase his technical proficiency in music, a practice he continued up to a year before his death—a humbling thought. Every year a new musical emerged from his pen, usually in collaboration with his brother Ira. The list is impressive: *Tip Toes* (1925), *Oh Kay!* (1926), *Funny Face* (1927), *Rosalie* (1929), *Show Girl* (1929), *Girl Crazy* (1930), *Of Thee I Sing* (1931), *Pardon My English* (1933), and more. *Of Thee I Sing* won him the Pulitzer Prize in 1931.

As a song writer he matched the greatest names of the industry, such as Berlin, Kern and Porter. Such popular songs as 'I got rhythm' (1930) taken from the show *Girl Crazy*, or 'Nice work if you can get it' (1937), illustrate his ability to blend the popular musical style with jazz in an immediately attractive and yet sophisticated fashion.

Parallel to his 'light' music activities, he continued to write concert works in the vein of *Rhapsody in Blue*. Encouraged by the success of this work, Gershwin turned to an even more ambitious work, a full-scale Piano Concerto in F (1925). While both blues and jazz idioms dominate this work, it is unified by a rhapsodic cyclical treatment he had learned from nineteenth-century masters. In all three movements, the listener's interest is unfailingly maintained by Gershwin's melodic inventiveness which seems to pour forth with an effortless natural flow.

The *Three Piano Preludes* (1926) separate the piano concerto from his next major composition, the symphonic poem *An*

American in Paris (1928). A visit to Paris gave him the idea of
portraying an American visitor's impressions of the city while
exploring the streets. According to the composer, the work is 'a
rhapsodic ballet' which is left to the imagination of the listener
to visualise. Some of the impressions are made quite clear, such
as youthful abandon, strolling along the streets (in the spirit of
the more recent 'Singing in the Rain'), the tooting horns of
passing cars, and, of course, jazz music and the dancing of the
can-can at the Folies Bergère—these are all featured in this
entertaining musical homage to Paris.

Gershwin's *Second Rhapsody* (1931) has never achieved the
same popularity as *Rhapsody in Blue*. Yet, it is a worthy com-
panion to it, containing great rhythmic sophistication, emphasised by its substantial use of percussive instruments,
including the piano, and in its overall structure. Gershwin himself was certainly aware of its compositional merit and
regarded it as one of his best works. It seems that, like his
Cuban Overture, it remains to be re-discovered by the general
public. Originally titled *Rumba*, the *Cuban Overture* (1932) was
written in the same year as the *Second Rhapsody*, and it shares
with it an almost harsh and percussive sonority. As the title
suggests, it was written under the influence of a visit to
Havana where the composer heard and was fascinated by
Cuban music performed with special percussion instruments,
such as bongo and maracas.

In the *Variation on 'I Got Rhythm'* (1934) Gershwin took the
song from his show *Girl Crazy* and set it as a brilliant variation
for piano and orchestra. It is a short piece, but it reveals a virtuosity and a sure-handed compositional panache which is
deeply rooted in the jazz improvisational style.

The lives of black people as a subject in literature became
increasingly popular during the 1920s. Among several interesting publications, perhaps the most memorable was Eugene
O'Neill's play *The Emperor Jones* (1920), which was later
adapted for an opera by Louis Gruenberg (1889–1964) in 1933.
Another successful work which Gershwin read as early as 1926
was the novel *Porgy* by Du Bose Heyward (1885–1940). The
book interested Gershwin enough for him to write to the

author and suggest writing a 'folk' opera based on the story. The author agreed but it was not until 1933 that the work finally materialised, by which time the Heywards had made a stage adaptation of the novel. The libretto of the opera, as so many times before, were written by Ira Gershwin in collaboration with Heyward.

Porgy and Bess (1935) is in three acts and involves a large cast with seven black protagonists. In essence the story is about a tragic relationship between Porgy, a crippled beggar, and Bess, a woman of easy virtue. Porgy murders Bess's lover, Crown and while Porgy is with the police, Bess is tempted to follow another man called Sporting Life, who is a 'happy dust' (a drug dealer). She goes with him to New York and when Porgy returns he learns what has happened and decides to follow them to find his beloved Bess. The subject is treated with vitality and compassion.

This is a full-scale opera but without arias in the conventional sense. Instead Gershwin used show-tunes, spirituals, blues and so forth, and all to great effect. The opera is full of memorable melodies, such as 'Summertime', 'I got plenty o' nuttin'', 'It ain't necessarily so', 'Bess, oh where's my Bess' and 'Oh Lord, I'm on my way'. In stature *Porgy and Bess* stands in the history of American opera as Mussorsgsky's *Boris Godunov* does in Russian opera and Alban Berg's *Wozzeck* does in Austrian. It also shares with them a somewhat isolated place in the history of opera outside the mainstream. Nevertheless, they are singular masterpieces of the repertoire.

When writing *Porgy and Bess* Gershwin was at the peak of his creative power. Tragically, he died of a brain tumour in 1937 before he reached forty. His impact upon music was such that his influence was felt among such diverse composers as Ravel and Bernstein as well as in the world of song writers and contemporary musicals. However, perhaps his greatest influence was upon the music-loving public who have continued to love his music by playing and listening to it.

5
The Romantics at Heart:
Carl Ruggles, Walter Piston, Virgil Thomson, Roy Harris and Samuel Barber

Music that does not surge is not great music
Carl Ruggles

I N SPITE OF THEIR MARKED DIFFERENCES, THE composers in this chapter nevertheless share a tendency which in one way or another manifests itself through traditional European influences. Neo-classicism with a romantic expressionism, a mystical relationship with nature or religion and, apart from Ruggles, a tonally orientated musical style all figure in the work of these composers.

Carl Ruggles (1876–1971)

By training and inclination Carl Ruggles was a violinist but he also studied theory and composition with some distinguished teachers. He even found time to study English literature at Harvard University and before settling down to a teaching career, he worked as an engraver in Boston. As well as writing music criticism, he took up conducting, a career he successfully followed for eleven years in Winona, Minnesota. In 1917 he moved to New York, in the hope of finding some recognition as a composer. There, he took part the activities of the International Composers' Guild, one of the most forward-looking institutions of its kind. Between 1920 and 1943, while he taught composition, he took his annual holidays in Vermont and eventually settled there. In largely self-imposed isolation, he composed, though most of his energies were devoted to painting landscapes which he did in an expressionistic style.

Carl Ruggles was a contemporary of Ives and, like him, was a New Englander. But Ruggles differed dramatically from Ives both in drive and in spirit. He shared with Schoenberg, a contemporary of both Americans, a lugubrious and intense expressionistic temperament. Without knowing of Schoenberg's own evolution from the late romantic style to 'free atonal' expressionism, Ruggles developed his own atonal expressionism in isolation. Whereas Schoenberg's expressionism contains an element of aggression from his polemical stance, Ruggles, a mystic and hermit by inclination, turned to nature not so much for consolation but to lose himself within it. His music is an expressionistic manifestation of his sense of human insignificance and is characterised by heroic struggles made poignant by this mystical wonder in the face of the unknown. In the score of *Portals* (1926), written for string orchestra, Ruggles copied a quotation from Whitman, "What are those of the known but to ascend and enter into the unknown", revealing what he had in mind and the often ascending structure of his melodies are the musical equivalent of this striving towards a universal mystery.

During his long lifetime he composed only a handful of works of which few are likely to be heard. *Angels* (1920–1921) for four trumpets and three trombones (originally for six trumpets) is written in an extremely dissonant contrapuntal style dominated by minor seconds and ninths as well as major sevenths, so characteristic of atonal expressionism. Yet the music succeeds in conveying something of an angelic ecstasy through its instrumental vocalization. *Vox clamans in deserto* (*Voice crying in the desert*) from 1923 and written for solo voice, chorus and orchestra, is a setting of three poems— 'Parting at Morning' by Robert Browning, 'Son of Mine' by Meltzer and 'A Clear Night' by Whitman. It is a work of great intensity and beauty. In the profound *Man and Mountains* (1924), William Blake's vision was the inspiring force: "Great things are done when men and mountains meet". Originally written for a small orchestra, it was revised for a large one in 1936. Its three movements are entitled 'Men', 'Lilacs' and 'Marching Mountains'.

Perhaps his most familiar work is the short symphonic

poem *Suntreader* (1926–1931). This is an intense composition in which the string melody is particularly dominant. The motto from Browning, "Sun-treader—life and light be thine forever", reveals something of the composer's intentions and the sense of an exalted vision. The style of the music is one of the best examples of Ruggles's atonal romantic expressionism. *Evocations* (1937–1943) and four chants for piano solo are brief utterances in which contrapuntal devices, such as canonic writing so much liked by Webern, are employed.

From the first composition he allowed to be published, 'Toys' (1919), a song based on one of his own poems, to his last work, *Organum for orchestra* (1944–1947), Ruggles showed an obsessively self-critical mind. His self-doubt not only forced him constantly to revise the few works he wrote, but it also led him to destroy others, including an opera. Many critics have appraised his small output as having a quality of concentration. One of Ruggles's champions, Charles Seeger, has suggested that Ruggles could have written more, if only the circumstances had been better. Be that as it may, he would surely have had the same obsessive nature and his creative power, which cannot be denied, may well have been intrinsically limited.

Walter Piston (1894–1976)

Walter Piston was of Italian origin and at first was a promising painting student at the Massachusetts Normal Art School. In 1916, after graduating, he took up the study of music in earnest, enrolling at Harvard in 1920. In the same year he also married his fellow art student, Kathryn Nason. After his graduation in 1924, he went to France for a period of two years on a travel scholarship. In Paris he studied with Paul Dukas (1865–1935), the composer of the famous *L'Apprenti Sorcier*, at the École Normal de Musique. He also studied privately with Nadia Boulanger (1887–1979), who was developing something of an industry in teaching Americans in France.

On his return to America in 1926 he joined the music staff at

Harvard University. With this began a distinguished academic career which ended with his retirement in 1960. His contribution to the teaching of music spread well beyond his country as did his didactic writings on music. *Harmonic Analysis* (1933), *Harmony* (1941), *Counterpoint* (1947) and *Orchestration* (1955) all became familiar text books among music students on both sides of the Atlantic.

As a composer he remained a conservative modernist in whose music an elegant equilibrium was found between traditional Austro-German academic standards and the French-influenced intellectual ésprit. He remained largely untouched by folk-music and the cultivation of Americanism in music. In fact, he wrote that "The major problem for the composer must be to preserve and develop his individuality. He must resist the constant temptation to follow this or that fashion." He disliked the idea of American music as such, as he believed that American music is what American composers wrote in general and not what some were trying to make American by the use of nationalistic idioms. In his work the influence of Stravinsky, and above all the French school of modern composers from Fauré to Poulenc, can be detected. The tone which he strikes is international rather than American in the narrow sense of the word. His masterly neo-classical style with a romantic leaning could be defined as being to America what Benjamin Britten and Sergei Prokofiev are to their respective countries, but with one major difference, as Piston was an almost entirely instrumental composer.

Between 1937 to 1965, he wrote eight symphonies of substantial size and of memorable quality. They are all based on the traditional symphonic plan and on tonal juxtaposition and gravitation. At the same time their neo-classical but easily assimilated modernism, makes them contemporary expressions. His diatonic melodies are classically pure and very singable. It was not for Piston to posture and project his will to achieve greatness with emotive extra musical references to great ideas. One could say, his music is for those who can appreciate the art of sound for its own sake. Thus, in connection with his fourth symphony, which was commissioned by the University of Minnesota in 1950, he wrote that it was "melodic and expressive and perhaps nearer than any of my other works to the solution of the problem of balance between expression and formal design". Although the headings of the four movements of this symphony—'Piacevole' (Peacefully), 'Ballando' (the composer called it "a dancing movement"), 'Contemplativo' and 'Energico'—refer to moods and tempi, the listener is left to absorb the music in terms of its musical logic and ingenuity rather than being stirred by extra musical images. Piston achieved in his eight symphonies a balance of feeling and form. Unpretentiousness, good humour and crafts-manship characterise both his life and work. Why these fine symphonies are hardly ever performed is a question which only the business world of the concert agencies can answer.

He also wrote several concertos, some of neo-classical con-certo grosso style, such as Concerto for Orchestra (1933), and some in the traditional solo concerto style such as Violin Concertos no. 1 (1939) and no. 2 (1960), Viola Concerto (1957), and others for flute, for clarinet and for two pianos. An inter-esting and unusual concerto experiment is his String Quartet Concerto (1976), for string quartet, wind and percussion. As a chamber music composer his contribution was also substan-tial, his five string quartets being outstanding. Ironically, and perhaps unfortunately, his most popular composition is still the suite taken from the ballet *The Incredible Flutist* (1938), which was a rare excursion from purely instrumental writing.

Piston's importance both as a teacher and composer can only be assessed in the light of civilisation and the transmis-sion of values. He was a civilising force, who, with a donnish elegance (hardly in existence nowadays), managed to reconcile past and present with an unpretentious intellectual integrity which was both illuminating and persuasive.

Virgil Thomson

Virgil Thomson (1896–1986), born in Kansas City, Missouri, was trained as a pianist and an organist, but his studies were interrupted by the First World War. He was scheduled to be sent to France for military service just as the war ended. Instead, he encountered French culture at Harvard. There he was introduced to French music by dedicated Francophile lecturers, among whom the most influential was, perhaps, S. Foster Damon, who, apart from being a scholar, was also a composer and a poet. Foster Damon introduced Thomson to the music of Eric Satie (1866–1925) and to the work of the Pennsylvanian born avant-garde novelist and poet Gertrude Stein (1874–1946). They in turn influenced Thomson's style. In 1921 he left for Paris where, like Piston, he became a pupil of Nadia Boulanger, the outstanding teacher/conductor who, through her teaching, made such a profound impression on several American composers. Thomson settled in Paris in 1925, where he stayed until the outbreak of the Second World War. It was during this time that he emerged as a fully-fledged composer.

While Thomson's musical style is deeply rooted in his American background, combining Southern Baptist hymn-singing with ragtime and popular songs, his strong affiliation with French musical culture moulded his musical thinking to a large extent. It is by no means an over-statement to say that he absorbed the music of Satie, 'Les Six' and the neo-classicism of Stravinsky to such a degree that his music became an American off-shoot of largely French neo-classical music of the 1920s and 1930s. Yet his individuality as an American composer is never in question as it is securely founded on the values of his native land. In later years he evolved a lyrical neo-romantic voice which matched well his deliberate stylistic simplicity, something that he largely learned from Satie and Poulenc. This style served him well in his sustained interest in writing sacred music and could be seen as a continuation of what Satie was hinting at in his *Messe des pauvres* and, to a certain extent, *Socrate*. Indeed, Thomson's wit and a well-developed sense of humour permeate even some of his sacred compositions.

His earlier works show his interest in nineteenth-century American popular music, as well as in certain traditional forms such as the tango and the waltz. *Two Sentimental Tangos* (1923) for piano, the *Sonata da Chiesa* (1926) for clarinet, trumpet, viola, horn and trombone (of which the second movement is a tango), *Synthetic Waltzes* (1925) for four hands, no. 8 of the Ten Piano Etudes (1943–1944) and *The Major La Guardia Waltzes* (1942) for orchestra all illustrate his sustained preoccupation with dance forms.

His first symphony, *Symphony on a Hymn Tune* (1926–1928), was one of his most remarkable creations of the period. Evoking nineteenth-century American farming life of the Midwest, the spirit of Baptist worship also permeates the work. Symphony no. 2 (1931) lacks the halo of the earlier symphony but shares with it Thomson's use of folk materials on which both works are based. Symphony no. 3 (1972) has failed to make the impact it deserves.

Unlike Ruggles, Thomson was a strikingly versatile and prolific composer in both orchestral, chamber and vocal music. During his long life he wrote in most musical forms including the concerto, a popular example being his Concerto for Cello and Orchestra (1949).

Equally successful are his choral works, as is convincingly illustrated by his *Stabat Mater* (1931) for soprano and string quartet, and the tongue-in-cheek *Missa pro defunctis* (1960), where a collage and parody technique is used by incorporating both sacred and secular music (e.g. hymns and waltzes).

His chamber music includes two string quartets, written in 1931 and 1932, which both use the waltz, so much liked by Thomson. Several more chamber music compositions such as *Five Portraits for Four Clarinets* (1929), an unusual combination for this instrument, and the Violin Sonata (1930–1931), are distinguished works.

Being a pianist and an organist, he composed a considerable corpus for both instruments. One should remember that in his youth he was a practising church organist, and played the piano for silent films. Among his piano compositions, the most striking are his humourous *Portraits*, largely inspired by Gertrude Stein's own *Portraits*. He also wrote portraits for other instrumental combinations, such as *Portraits for Violin Alone* (1928–1940). Among his organ works are *Variations on Sunday*

School Tunes (1926–1927) in which Gospel hymns form the basis of four sets of variations: 'Come ye disconsolate', 'There's not a friend like the lowly Jesus', 'Will there be any stars in my crown?' and 'Shall we gather at the river?'. These are an outstanding contribution to the repertoire.

While in France, Thomson had the opportunity of forming friendships with Jean Cocteau, André Gide, Ernest Hemingway, Pablo Picasso and Gertrude Stein. Apart from Satie and other leading French composers of the period, it was the encounter with Gertrude Stein which proved to be particularly fruitful for him. They met in Paris in 1925 and Thomson became one of the many expatriate artists who joined her circle of friends. Music was not her forte but she was flattered by Thomson's interest in her poems, several of which he set to music. They decided to collaborate on an opera with a Spanish location. The result of their collaboration was *Four Saints in Three Acts* (1928), a surrealist operatic romp with a nonsense text, such as the notorious aria 'Let lucy lili lili lucy lucy let lucy lucy lili lili lili lili'. Humorously sub-titled as an 'Opera to be sung' it features two Spanish saints, Teresa and Ignatus Loyola, and the fictitious Saint Chavez and Saint Settlement. To give a taste of the style, in one scene in the first act, Saint Ignatus not only serenades Saint Teresa, but gallantly offers her a bunch of flowers. The opera contains no real story but rather a series of happenings under the following headings:

Prelude	A narrative of Prepare for Saints
Act 1	Saint Teresa half indoors and half out of doors
Act 2	Might it be mountains if it were not Barcelona
Act 3	Saint Ignatus and one of two literally
Act 4	The sisters and saints reassembled and re-enacting why they went away to stay.

Its first performance was given in 1936 under the auspices of the Society of Friends and Enemies of Modern Music. The production was staged by Sir Frederick Ashton and was performed by black singers. It was an enormous success.

The Second World War separated them for five years. In 1945 Ashton and Thomson met again for another operatic collaboration, *The Mother of Us All* (1947). Gertrude Stein completed the libretto just before her death in 1946. The opera, premièred in 1947, has as its heroine the American feminist Susan B. Anthony. The composer thought that his score was something of a "memory-book" in which can be found ". . . a souvenir of all those sounds and kinds of tunes that were once the music of rural America." It is an evocative work which has not lost any of its appeal even after four decades. Sadly, these two immensely entertaining operas are largely neglected today.

Thomson also made a reputation as an outstanding composer of film music. In these scores he projected his American roots by deliberately using native music. The score for *The Plow that Broke the Plain* (1936) is based on cowboy songs, *The River* (1937) on spirituals, *Tuesday in November* (1945) on hymns and waltzes, and in *The Louisiana Story* (1948), believed by some to be among his finest scores, he used Arcadian songs and dances. The composer arranged an orchestral suite of four movements for concert performance. Viewed nostalgically through the eyes of a child, the documentary film is about the development of the oil industry and its effect on the Bayou country. As the headings of each movement of the suite indicate—Pastoral, Chorale, Passacaglia and Fugue—this work possesses a neo-classical structure. Yet the discrete Thomsonian lyrical romanticism which he so craftily evolved during the years is also evident in its gentle longing tone.

Finally, tribute is also due to this versatile man's ability as a writer. His unpretentious autobiography *Virgil Thomson* (1966) makes fascinating reading. So does his earlier *The State of Music* (1939), and *Music Right and Left* (1951). A selection of his music criticism, *Music Reviewed, 1940–1954*, was published in 1967. This collection shows his brilliance as a critic who wrote with wit and in an attractive style, indefatigably defending the cause of modern music. *American Music Since 1910* (1971), his book on the American musical scene, though well-informed, is strangely unfocused and chatty. This may be because of the difficulty in writing a history of an art when the author himself plays a major role in it. Moreover, there is a note of jealousy in his comments about the belated success of Charles Ives. Poking fun with Gertrude Stein's famous line "A rose is a rose, is a rose", "A genius is a genius, is a genius". Perhaps Thomson could not help resenting the powerful influence of Ives, which is rather mean for someone with such immense talent as Virgil Thomson.

Roy Harris

When Roy Harris (1898–1979) was still a child, his family moved from Oklahoma to California following their fortunes as farmers. Like so many American artists of the time, he too was drawn to France and the classes of Nadia Boulanger, which he joined in 1926. While in Paris, he wrote the Concerto for Piano, and the Clarinet and String Quartet (1926) as well as the first version of *Whitman Triptych* (1927). This great American poet had a major influence on Harris, who on several occasions set his poems to music.

A spinal injury forced him to return to America where he lived on the fees of university and college lectureships as well as on several scholarships which he was awarded in recognition of his art. At sixty, he became the cultural ambassador of his country to the Soviet Union. He endearingly admitted that the injury was a blessing in disguise, as it forced him to compose away from the piano. This he found liberating as it enabled him to develop his aural imagination and above all his polyphonic thinking.

Temperamentally as well as philosophically he was a conservative who believed that music has been steadily declining since Beethoven's time and that the 'rock-bottom' was reached with Stravinsky and Schoenberg (it is worth noting that the two compositions which he cites as having reached to lowest level were *Le Sacre du printemps* and *Pierrot Lunaire*). Thus not only did he frown at modernism, but also the nineteenth-century romantic period, which was seen by Harris as an unfortunate detour from a historical development which reached its climax with Bach and Mozart. According to Harris, Beethoven's work was already questionable. Harris, with romantic nostalgia, clearly regretted the fact that nineteenth-century romanticism and modernism had ever developed and instead wanted to resurrect a golden age in musical tradition which, according to him, had come to a close after Beethoven's death. In the light of this, it is hard to imagine that Harris's music has anything to do with our century. Yet, it is contemporary just as much as the music of Jean Sibelius and Edmund Rubbra was contemporary.

The Americanness of Harris's music is established by his frequent references to American subject matters. For example, his Symphony no. 4 (1940), *The Folk Symphony*, is founded on old American songs. His Symphony no. 10 (1965) is a symphonic and programmatic evocation of Abraham Lincoln's life. His melodies, not unlike those of Sibelius, are widely spaced and invoke nature. His harmony is firmly based on tonality, but with a personal interpretation of the relationships of overtones. He did not embark, however, on a didactic system, like Hindemith. Contrapuntal thinking predominates his works in which he incorporated canonic and fugal devices. Structurally, he likes telescoping into one movement the traditional multi-movement symphonic form of the classical composers, as in his Symphony no. 7. Ironically this is an idea which he has borrowed from the nineteenth century, above all from Liszt. He also preferred to employ what can be best described as a seed technique, that is, the method of allowing a musical idea to germinate and grow into a whole musical world—a concept that Beethoven exploited.

One of his deservedly popular works is his Symphony no. 3 of 1938. The programme note given by the composer gives an insight into his thinking in this symphony:

> Section I. Tragic—low string sonorities. Section II. Lyric -strings, horns, woodwinds. Section III. Pastoral—woodwinds with a polytonal string background. Section IV. Fugue—dramatic. A. Brass and percussion predominating. B. Canonic development of materials from Section II constituting background for further development of fugue. C. Brass climax, rhythmic motif derived from fugue subject. Section V. Dramatic—tragic. A. Restatement of violin theme of Section I; tutti strings in canon with tutti woodwinds against brass and percussion developing rhythmic motif from Section IV. B. Coda—development of materials from Section I and II over pedal timpani.

The symphony is in one continuous movement and is based on folk-like and hymn-like melodies. Harris absorbed the American vernacular style to such an extent that it was not necessary for him to quote specific folk or hymn tunes directly, unless he wanted to, as he could readily make up his own in the appropriate style.

Harris was a distinguished symphonist whose Symphony no. 3 is a fine monument to his art. One could argue, however, that hailing him as one of the most important modern symphonists was as an exaggerated claim as that similarly made of Sibelius in Great Britain. The fact that Harris's Symphony no. 3 was the first American symphony to be conducted by Toscanini is indeed a compliment but it is also revealing in view of the conductor's conservatism.

Samuel Barber

It is not by accident that in 1938 the twenty-eight year old Samuel Barber (1910–1981) became the first ever American composer whose music was to be part of a concert programme played by the NBC Symphony Orchestra under Toscanini. The composer's works were the *Adagio for Strings* (1936), a warmly lyrical piece of music which Barber adapted from the slow movement of his String Quartet in B Minor (1936), and *Essay no. 1 for Orchestra* (1937). To this day it is largely on the elegiac *Adagio* that Barber's popularity with the general public rests.

The *Essay no. 2 for Orchestra* (1942), on the other hand, was given its debut by Bruno Walter. The significance of mentioning these two eminent conductors' involvement with Barber's music is that they more or less dominated musical taste in America for a considerable period. Their attitude towards modern music was largely echoed by the general public—they wanted modernity, or modernism, without tears. The music of both Harris and Barber fitted this requirement. Barber adhered unquestioningly to classical forms and filled them with his personal feelings and thoughts. As Barber himself has stated: "I just go on doing, as they say, my thing". His harmonic thinking, like Piston's and Harris's, remained firmly tonal and he even maintained the traditional key relationships. Stylistically he is neither a neo-romantic nor a neo-classicist, but rather his music is an unproblematical continuation of late romantic musical procedures as applied by a highly civilised American internationalist. But, within the conservative idiom which he chose, he created a body of works which proves what Schoenberg stressed once in connection with tonality, that many masterpieces can yet be written in C major.

His interest in English poetry resulted in a body of songs, including *Dover Beach* (1931), a setting of the poem by Matthew Arnold, *Music for a Scene from Shelley* (1933) based on Shelley's *Prometheus Unbound*, *Three Songs* (1936) from James Joyce's *Chamber Music*, *Hermit Songs* (1953) based on Medieval Irish texts dating from the eighth to the thirteenth centuries, and several more settings including some of Robert Graves's poems and 'Solitary Hotel', from Joyce's *Ulysses*. In all these songs, it is apparent that Barber was a professionally trained singer by his sympathetic understanding of the human voice.

Of his three orchestral essays, the last one, the third *Essay*, was composed as late as 1978, in which Barber introduced the idea of writing a musical composition in the same analytical and logical manner as the unfolding of an idea in literature. These are attractive orchestral compositions which are likely to remain in the concert repertoire.

In the concerto form, he wrote three works, the Violin Concerto (1939), the Cello Concerto (1945) and the Piano Concerto (1962). These are all, because of their uncomplicated modernism, easily approachable.

His operatic ventures, *Vanessa* (1956–1957) and *Anthony and Cleopatra* (1966), probably because of the composer's lack of real inspiration and because the revival of French grand opera style was out of touch with the period, were not well received and never established themselves in the operatic repertory.

Of all the composers discussed in this chapter, it was Barber who was perhaps the most conventional, but in his songs and in *Prayers of Kierkegaard* (1954) for soprano solo, chorus and orchestra, his voice was at its most inspired.

6
Baked by Nadia Boulanger:
Aaron Copland

Is the Dust Bowl more American than, say, a corner in the Boston Athenaeum?
Walter Piston

ARON COPLAND (1900–1981) WAS BORN IN Brooklyn, New York. His parents were Russian Jews who emigrated to America during the last quarter of the nineteenth century and his father, Harris Copland, was eventually elected president of the synagogue in Brooklyn. This background had its impact on Aaron Copland who was to incorporate Jewish elements into his music, elements that are directly related to the cantations of the Jewish synagogue, as can be heard, for example, in the piano trio *Vitebsk* (1929). Wilfrid Mellers has pointed out, in his book *Man and His Music*, ". . . that both Negro and Jew are dispossessed peoples who become, for Copland, symbolic of urban man's uprootedness".[1]

In 1920 the urge to study in Paris made the young composer leave for France, where he enrolled at the newly founded American Conservatory in Fontainebleau. Copland was lured, like so many American composers, into the classes of the charismatic teacher, Nadia Boulanger. It was she, who during the four years of his apprenticeship in her 'boulangerie' widened his horizon to include European music. It was also she, who perhaps unwittingly, awakened a sense of frustration in Copland regarding the state of art music in America and kindled in him a desire to find his own American voice, just as his European contemporaries had found theirs. He began to focus on the harmonic, melodic, and above all, rhythmic characteristics of blues and jazz.

His *Symphony for Organ and Orchestra* (1924) paid homage to his teacher who had commissioned it for her American concert tour. This work brought to the 1920s an idea that had already been tested by Camille Saint-Saëns (1835–1921) in his Symphony no. 3 in C minor (1889) in which the organ plays a prominent role. A much more promising composition was, however, his suite *Music for the Theatre* (1925), where his interest in blues and jazz and the influence of Stravinsky gained expression. His grandiose tendencies were suppressed in this piece with economy and wit. A more ambitious composition followed suit, in which a jazz style, adapted to the concert hall, was again pursued in the Piano Concerto (1926).

1930 signalled a turning point in Copland's life, as he adopted a more rigorous style of writing. An outstanding composition of this period in his *Piano Variations* (1930). This ten-minute composition contains nineteen variations and a finale. It is striking in its harsh sonorities and in the density of its writing. In style it is astonishingly advanced and is close to the expressionism of Schoenberg and Webern. Its quasi-serial motto theme comprises four notes: E—C—D—C. The *Piano Variations* were followed by a few further compositions in a similarly lean style: *Short Symphony* (1932–1933), this later was arranged as a brilliant *Sextet* (1937) for clarinet, piano and string quartet; and *Statement for Orchestra* (1932–1935). None of these, however, match the power of the *Piano Variations* which opened Copland's second musical phase in 1930.

Suddenly, he changed tune again, as it were, by turning away from eccentric avant-garde music and started instead to cultivate a good-humoured, energetic and plainly nationalistic popular style with the aim of bridging the gap between the modern composer and his audience. He not only wooed his public with music that was immediately appealing, but he also involved himself with several national and international conferences, taking part in leagues, festivals, publishing and teaching. He carried on with these during the best part of his life, indefatigably busying himself for the cause of American music. His determined ideological involvement even led him during the 1940s to semi-official diplomatic work in fostering a good relationship with Latin America which he visited on several occasions from 1932 onwards. His encounter with

Latin America, especially his visit to Mexico, left a deep impression on Copland and he put this experience to good use in several of his compositions. His change of style and the influence of Latin America which occurred at the same time was by no means a fruitless coincidence. One of the first successes in his modern-music-made-popular style was *El Salón México* (1933–1936), which brought him renewed recognition. This vigorous orchestral piece was inspired by a painting of a dance hall and based on popular Mexican tunes. Its première in Mexico City was conducted by the famous Mexican composer Carlos Chavez in 1937. The idea of adopting American folk tunes in a fashion similar to *El Salon Mexico* soon followed. Cowboy songs were the basis of the two ballets *Billy the Kid* (1938) and *Rodeo* (1942). These works were founded on rather primitive stories and the music is appositely like film music, differing from the typical Hollywood style in its debt to American folk melodies and to the rhythmic style of Stravinsky, rather than on the verve of Tchaikovsky and Rachmaninov, while nevertheless pouring forth with the bitter-sweet taste of saccharin.

Perhaps the most notorious of his popularising and utility works was *Lincoln Portrait* (1942) for narrator and orchestra. The narrator reads from Lincoln's letters and speeches while the music gives way to grand patriotic emotions including quotations from a folk ballad 'Springfield Mountain' and a song from Stephen Foster's 'Camptown Races'. Though doubtlessly carried out with noble intentions, it is no more than competently written patriotic propaganda not unlike any Russian counterpart of the 1940s and 1950s. Also belonging to this genre and written in the same year is the *Fanfare for the Common Man* commissioned by Eugene Goosens.

In the early forties, Martha Graham commissioned Copland to write a ballet for her company. The subject of *Appalachian Spring* (1943–1944), as this ballet was to be called, was a Shaker wedding in the Appalachian mountains. It was first performed in 1945 and its suite version won the Pulitzer Prize. The work turned out to be one of Copland's most lyrical compositions. It contains eight sections which are played without breaks. The composer gave the following verbal indications:

1. Very slowly. Introduction of the characters, one by one, in a suf-
fused light.
2. Fast. Sudden burst of unison strings in A major arpeggios starts
the action. A sentiment both elated and religious gives the
keynote of this scene.
3. Moderate. Duo for the Bride and her Intended—scene of ten-
derness and passion.
4. Quite fast. The Revivalist and his flock—Folksy feelings—sug-
gestions of square dance and country fiddlers.
5. Still faster. Solo dance of the Bride—presentiment of mother-
hood. Extremes of joy and fear and wonder.
6. Very slowly (as at first). Transition scenes reminiscent of the
introduction.
7. Calm and flowing. Scenes of daily activity for the Bride and her
farmer-husband. There are five variations on a Shaker theme. The
theme, sung by a solo clarinet, was taken from a collection of
Shaker melodies compiled by E. D. Andrews, and published later
under the title The Gift to be Simple. The melody I borrowed and
used almost literally, is called 'Simple Gifts' . . .
8. Moderate. Coda. The Bride takes her place among her neigh-
bours. At the end the couple are left 'quiet and strong in their new
home'. Muted strings intone a hushed, prayerlike passage. The
close is reminiscent of the opening music.

There can be no doubt about Copland's craftsmanship in this
or in any other of his compositions. Yet, a comparison with
Stravinsky's *Les Noces* (1921–1923) is inevitable, as it must have
been Copland's model for *Appalachian Spring*. The resemblance
lies both in subject matter and dramatic structure. For example,
in their respective finales, the couples in both Stravinsky's and
Copland's works are alone in the sanctity of their privacy. But
whereas Stravinsky's *Les Noces* is one of his greatest ritualistic
sound visions, Copland's *Appalachian Spring* is a professionally
written lyrical entertainment. In contrasting these two works,
one can see the difference between genius and talent, however
great the latter may be.

Apart from *The Second Hurricane* (1936), which was conceived as an opera for children, Copland only wrote one opera,
The Tender Land (1952–1954). Horace Everett's love story, on
which it is based, takes place in the farming community of the
Midwest during the 1930s. At the climax of the opera, the girl,

Laurie, is abandoned by her lover Martin, and she then decides to give up everything in order to search for him. In this work too the composer chose simple and immediate tunes which are backed by a more sophisticated orchestration. As with *Appalachian Spring*, it is difficult not to make a comparison in this case with the climax of Gershwin's *Porgy and Bess*. There too, one of the lovers is abandoned (although the genders are reversed) and then decides to follow the other. It is often the case in art that one good idea, which has worked well, is subsequently taken up by a series of other artists. Copland and Everett in this case are walking in the shadow of Gershwin's *Porgy and Bess*, which is much the more substantial work of the two. Not even Copland's forte, the use of energetic dances, gives real spark to *The Tender Land*.

There is hardly any form of music which Copland did not touch upon with great energy and compositional skill. His range includes film scores, such as the music written for the film adaptation of Steinbeck's *Of Mice and Men* (1939) and *The Red Pony* (1948), and song settings such as his arrangements of the two volumes of *Old American Songs*. His skill in song writing is especially evident in his sympathetic handling of *12 Poems* (1944–1945), settings of one of the most remarkable of American poets, Emily Dickinson.

In his indefatigable work as composer, teacher and organiser, he even found time to write about music. His most popular publication is *What to Listen for in Music* (1939), but the others are also full of interest: *The New Music: 1900–1960* (1968) (which was originally published as *Our New Music* in 1941), *Music and Imagination* (1952), which contains six Norton lectures given at Harvard University in 1951–1952 and *Copland on Music* (1960), a collection of essays.

For decades Copland dominated the American scene, or at least that is what one was made to believe outside America, whether by the press or by himself. He has on occasion been referred to as the 'Ambassador of American music', 'The dean of American music', and also 'the spiritual father to an entire generation of American composers'. His personal zest and influence were certainly considerable during his lifetime, but one could argue that it was a loss to music when he abandoned his 'second period' in favour of an aggressively projected style of popular appeal. He neither shared Gershwin's natural feel for popular melody, as he was seldom at his best with lyrical passages, nor did he possess Ives's instinctive visionary genius. It is more than likely that his future standing as a composer will fall considerably below some of those whom he overshadowed during his lifetime.

7
A Frenchman in New York:
Edgard Varèse

My experimenting is done before I make the music. Afterwards it is the listener who must experiment.
Edgard Varèse

VARÈSE (1883–1965) WAS FRENCH BY BIRTH, BUT IN his early thirties he adopted America as his home and eventually took up American citizenship in 1926. His childhood and years of apprenticeship as a musician were spent in Europe. He had a thorough training at the Schola Cantorum under such distinguished composers and teachers as Vincent D'Indy (1851–1931) and Albert Roussel (1869–1937). He also studied at the Paris Conservatory with the famous organist and composer Charles Widor (1844–1937). Becoming a musician was not, however, as straightforward as those few lines about his background would indicate. His father wanted him to take the engineering course at the École Polytechnique and was against him becoming a musician. Varèse stuck to his choice of music as a career and even left the family home in order to follow his vocation.

His reading of Ferruccio Busoni's (1866–1924) progressive declarations on new music, *Sketch for a New Aesthetic of Music* (1907), galvanised the young composer into seeking new vistas and friendships and above all into forging an independent voice as a composer. He shared Busoni's belief that creation lay in "making laws, not in following laws ready-made". In 1907 he moved to Berlin where he quickly established himself as a musician. He founded and conducted a choir, the Symphonische Chor, and he had the good fortune to be associated not only with Busoni, but also with Gustav Mahler, Richard Strauss, Max Reinhardt and Hugo Hofmannstal among other eminent figures. Hofmannstal even gave him permission to use

his *Oedipus und die Sphinx* for an opera. During his frequent
visits to Paris, he met Claude Debussy (1862–1918) and Eric
Satie (1866–1925) as well as the poet Guillaume Apollinaire
and the novelist Romain Rolland.

In 1913, while on a visit to France, most of his manuscripts
were lost in a fire in Berlin. He himself contributed further to
their loss by destroying more of his works which he found
unworthy of his ideals. The outbreak of the First World War
brought to an end a successful conducting tour with the Czech
Philharmonic Orchestra during which he gave the première of
the Suite version of Debussy's *Le Martyre de St Sebastien*.
Having joined the army, he was soon discharged on grounds of
ill health. Unable to find a permanent post, he left France for
America, initially to give a performance of Berlioz's *Requiem* in
New York, and settled there for good in 1915.

In a remarkable and informative book on Varèse written by
his second wife Louise Varèse, *A Looking-Glass Diary*, we learn
of his ambitions in America:

> Besides an adequate supply of money and an ample supply of
> introductions, Varèse brought to America two idées fixes: he would
> make his mark as a conductor and at the same time lots of money
> for his Claude adoré (his son); second, he would create the new
> instruments he needed for the music he was going to compose.[1]

Like most expatriates, or refugees, Varèse experienced the
daily pendulum swing between elation and hope and total
despair and rejection. His letters illustrate this state of mind:

> I believe that they are arranging for me to conduct a concert next
> month here at Carnegie Hall (which is the largest concert hall)
> with the New York Symphony Orchestra. If this is successful, it
> will be the foundation of my future. Things move slowly here—
> everyone is suspicious but once you're in the saddle the rest is
> generally clear sailing. I am full of courage, energy, determina-
> tion—I have something they don't have—so it is bound to go and
> will go. It only needs patience.[2]

Less than a fortnight later, having heard nothing positive about
the concert, he wrote:

> New York: banal city and dirty and the inhabitants handsome
> sportsman types—not more. I see only Europeans with whom

contact is possible. With the natives all conversation impossible no matter what the subject except the question of the 'Dollar', which is the only one that is of any interest or importance to them . . .[3]

Clearly it was not easy for Varèse, but his vigour, combined with his outstanding ability and a critical integrity, made him a prominent figure in American music relatively quickly, both as a conductor and composer. He also became known as the founder and musical director of the first modernist music society in America in 1921, the International Composers Guild (ICG). The manifesto published by the ICG stated:

The aim of the International Composers Guild is to centralise the works of the day, to group them in programs intelligently and organically constructed, and, with the disinterested help of singers and instrumentalists to present these works in such a way as to reveal their fundamental spirit.

During the six years of the Guild's existence, Varèse worked indefatigably for the promotion of modern compositions by giving concerts on a regular basis in which works of many contemporary composers, including Ruggles, Schoenberg and Webern were performed in New York for the first time. His aim through the ICG was to promote internationalism, but in order to promote American music he also founded the Pan American Society in 1926.

Earlier, he had also been involved with the founding of the short-lived New Symphony Orchestra, from which he resigned because the organisers wanted him to play less modern music. This was, of course, against his firmly held principles. His strong beliefs and his internationalism seem to have alienated some of his colleagues in the ICG. Some members, headed by Claire Reis (1888–1978), decided to form an alternative body under the name League of Composers, which, with its periodical *Modern Music* had a much longer life than the Guild. Nevertheless, it was Varèse who initiated the idea of promoting modern music in America in this fashion.

As a conductor, one of the many concerts he gave was a performance of Berlioz's Requiem Mass in New York in 1917. This coincided with America's mobilization for the war. The following year, he married the poet and translator Louise Norton.

In 1922, Varèse was in Berlin again where, together with Busoni, he founded the German equivalent of the ICG. At this time many similar societies were being formed and Varèse made contact with those in Moscow and Italy, the latter founded by the theorist and composer Alfredo Casella (1883–1947). Varèse contributed significantly to making the work of these societies internationally known.

As a composer, he turned away from his classical and romantic musical heritage. Bored with traditional music, he explored new possibilities which were even beyond the compositions of his contemporaries. He wanted new effects—he imagined sounds which not only encompassed noise as a legitimate vehicle for artistic statement, but also sounds which were extramusical, where acoustics and mathematics join forces with art in order to form a new expression. As he has stated:

> What we want is an instrument that will give us a continuous sound at any pitch. The composer and the electrician will have to labor together to get it. At any rate, we cannot keep on working in the old school colors. Speed and synthesis are characteristics of our epoch. We need twentieth century instruments to help us realize them in music.[5]

Electronically produced sounds were not available at this time and Varèse was conceptualising electronic music decades before it became possible. It would be a mistake, however, to think that because of his interest in the creative use of noise and other unconventional sound effects, he was allied to the creeds of the Cubists, Dadaists or Futurists. In spite of his association with Marcel Duchamp (1887–1968) and Francis Picabia (1897–1953)—he even contributed to Picabia's journal *391*— Varèse avoided becoming too involved with isms and systems; he preferred to stay on the fringe of these movements, retaining his individuality. He adhered to his own principle of 'organised sound'—organised not according to traditional principles but according to the mathematical logic of the pre-well-tempered Pythagorean concept of sound. He therefore also rejected the equally divided system of twelve semitones in an octave. He furthermore introduced the sustained use of noise, enhanced by his emphatic use of percussive instruments, which dominate his compositions, together with the idea of discarding traditional instruments in favour of newly-created ones—a development for which he had to wait for a long time.

His first major composition was *Ameriques* (1918–1921). Written for conventional instruments, it already shows Varèse's inclination towards percussive sonorities. The large orchestra, which includes eight horns and six trumpets, is further augmented by twenty-one percussion instruments, including a siren, a string drum—often referred to as 'lion's roar'—and a whip. These are played by an ensemble of ten players. The composer stressed that the title *Ameriques* was not so much ". . . purely geographic but . . . symbolic of discoveries—new worlds on earth, in the sky, or in the minds of men". The work is dedicated to two anonymous patrons who were helping Varèse during the writing of his composition. Rhythm, timbre and dynamics already dominate this composition in which traditional harmonic procedures are not used and in which melody in the conventional sense is more or less also discarded. The instrumental combinations and their progress in space and time make this work remarkable. Already in this early composition, Varèse was suggesting his alternative version to modern musical thinking, represented by Schoenberg and Stravinsky, by introducing what was then an unheard of dimension in sound—one that discards tonality or the chromatic negation of tonality altogether. This is a music of the present devoid of any nostalgic seeking for roots. Its starting point is to offer the experience, albeit still using conventional instruments, of a poetic realisation in 'organised sound' of the 'now' of this century.

Varèse's next composition, *Offrandes* (1921), uses two short South American poems, 'Chanson de la-hout' by the Chilean Vincente Huidobro and 'La Croix du Sud' by the Mexican Jose Juan Tablada. Originally entitled *Dedication*, one setting was dedicated to his wife and the other to his friend Carlos Salzado. These two surrealist poems are for soprano and chamber orchestra, but with the addition of eight percussion instruments as well as a harp. An extreme dynamic range and the extensive use of percussive sounds characterise this nevertheless lyrical piece of music. Poetic sound effects, such as at the end of the first poem, with the closing line "In her head a bird sings all year long", contrast with violent outbursts such as at the opening of the second poem, "Women with the gestures of the madrepore / Have hair and lips in orchid red".

After hearing *Offrandes*, Stravinsky reacted with the following good-humoured statement: ". . . the most extraordinary noise in all Varèse is the harp attack (heart attack, I almost said and that is what it almost gives one) at measure 17 in *La Croix du Sud* . . ."[6]

Hyperprism (1922–1923) was premièred in New York in the year it was completed and received its London debut the following year. It is written for a chamber ensemble consisting of piccolo, flute, clarinet, three horns, two trumpets, two trombones and an assortment of percussive instruments: sleigh bells, cymbals, crash cymbals, rattles, triangle, anvil, slapstick, Chinese blocks, tamtam, Indian drum, snare drum, bass drum, tambourine, siren and lion's roar. The title refers to a geometrical object in four dimensions. (In fact, most of Varèse's works have scientific names, but they work by association rather than having any strictly scientific meaning.) Urban life, or rather, urban sounds pervade this composition which conjures up an image of the city and clearly illustrates Varèse's increasing preoccupation with noise. Even the complex poly-rhythm comprise layer upon layer of depersonalised noise suggesting the violence of a mechanistic urban life and not the dance and trance-induced poly-rhythm of African and Oriental music used by his contemporaries. Whereas in *Ameriques* and *Offrandes*, the influence of Debussy is still strong, in *Hyperprism*, Varèse entered a domain entirely his own.

Varèse characteristically favoured the use of percussive instruments above all, not just for their rhythmic use, but equally for their predominantly pitchless noise quality. He particularly relied on woodwind and brass instruments as he disliked the strings for their vibrato and romantic quality.

Octandre (1923–1924) is a work written for flute, clarinet, oboe, bassoon, horn, trumpet, trombone and double bass. The title refers to flowers which have eight pollen-bearing organs. It is unique among Varèse's works with its semi-traditional, three (short) movement structure. There is , however, no real break between the second and third sections of the composition, so blurring the movements together. Melody-like utterances are also in evidence, in which the music of Stravinsky, in *Petrushka* for instance, can be recognised. But these aspects seem to diminish the otherwise brilliantly conceived sound effects of this short chamber composition. One could say, playing devil's advocate, that Varèse is least convincing when his music wanders into the domain of melody. His real strength is in composing musical statements which are the least melody orientated.

Integrales (1924–1925) represented a major step towards achieving what had preoccupied Varèse for some time—sound projection or spacial projection. These terms eventually were telescoped into the expression 'spacial music'. Much later the composer wrote: "*Integrales* was conceived for a spacial projection".[7] The basic idea of spacial music is to place the musicians in different areas either on the platform or indeed off it in order to give the feeling of distance or spacial separation to the sound effects. These can then be transmitted to the listeners in the same way as a beam of light or, as the composer put it, ". . . Probably I should call them beams of sound, since the feeling is akin to that aroused by beams of light sent forth by a powerful searchlight. For the ear—just as for the eye—it gives a sense of prolongation, a journey into space".[8] The instrumentation consists of two piccolos, two clarinets, an oboe, a horn, trumpet, piccolo trumpet, three trombones and seventeen percussion instruments. The percussion is divided into four groups: 1. suspended cymbal, side drum, tenor drum, snare drum; 2. castanets, cymbals, Chinese blocks; 3. sleigh bells, chains, tambourine, gong, tamtam; and 4. triangle, crash cymbal, rule, bass drum and slap-stick. It is astonishing to realise how far Varèse was able to achieve effects that would be readily available with electronic devices thirty years later.

His vast symphonic poem *Arcana* (1923–1927) refers to the

secret of nature sought by alchemists. Varèse had read *Hermetic Astronomy* by Paracelsus, the great Renaissance thinker and physician whose ideas were well ahead of his time in the treatment of diseases including mental illness, and quoted from it in the score of *Arcana*:

> One star exists higher than all the rest. This is the apocalyptical star; the second star is that of the ascendant. The third is that of the elements, and of these there are four, so that there is still another star, imagination, which begets a new star and a new heaven.

Varèse was, however, quick to point out that his composition was not in any way influenced by Paracelsus nor did he want to write a composition which would have reflected upon the semi-dedicatory text. But, in spite of the composer's efforts in trying to disassociate his work from Paracelsus, Odile Vivier made a convincing argument in finding a musical parallel in Varèse's compositional techniques and Paracelsus's preoccupation with the 'transmutation of elements':

> . . . Paracelsus, following the alchemists, describes the transmutation of elements. Varèse constructs his works in accordance with this principle: he attempts neither development nor transformation, but rather the transmutation of an initial cell or agglomeration, which he subjects to different tensions, different dynamics, and different gravitational functions in accordance with the attraction and density of further elements.[9]

Much later, in 1959, Varèse was to state:

> Concerning musical form as a resultant—the result of a process— I was struck by what seemed to me an analogy between the formation of my compositions and the phenomenon of crystallisation. There is an idea, the basis of an internal structure, expanding and split into different shapes or groups of sound constantly changing in shape, direction, and speed, attracted and repulsed by various forces. The form of a work is the consequence of this interaction. Possible musical forms are as limitless as the exterior forms of crystals. [10]

Arcana comprises one massive movement which is a crystallisation of his ideas in colliding sound blocks of enormous power. It is played by a very large orchestra, incorporating thirty-nine percussion instruments. It is a great piece of orchestral music, but with an arguable weakness in the melodic writing. Here too one is made aware of the influence of Stravinsky, not only rhythmically but also melodically. Whether this is conscious or not is difficult to say but motifs from *The Firebird*, *Petrushka*, and *The Rite of Spring* can be detected if only momentarily and then transmogrified into his own style.

The first performance of *Arcana* was conducted by Leopold Stokowski on 8 April 1927 in Philadelphia. The programme also included a recent work, *Ballet Mecanique* (1923–1925), by another American composer, George Antheil (1900–1959). Antheil too was influenced by and preoccupied with modern technology and gained some notoriety with works like *Airplane Sonata* for piano (1922). But the one work for which he is best remembered is the film score for the *Ballet Mecanique* which he created in collaboration with the painter Ferdinand Leger and the film producer Dudley Murphy. It was imaginative and courageous programming to perform *Arcana* and *Ballet Mecanique* together.

In October 1928, Varèse returned to Paris where he stayed until 1933. During that time he worked on one of his greatest compositions, *Ionization*. It calls for an ensemble of thirteen musicians who play two sirens, two tamtams, gong, crash cymbals, three bass drums, bongos, snare drums, quiros (from Cuba), slap-sticks, Chinese blocks, Cuban claves, triangle, maracas, sleigh bells, castanets, tambourine, anvil chimes, celesta and piano. Of these, only three instruments are capable of producing definite pitch: celesta, chimes and piano. These three are introduced only in the closing seventeen bars of the composition and their inclusion brings the work to its climax in a final glorification of sound energy which is, so to speak, the process of ionization.

This is the first Western composition in which percussion instruments alone are used. No other composer, including Milhaud and Stravinsky, had used a percussion ensemble in such a radical way. Varèse's music, as I have previously stated, has little to do with the assimilation of African or Oriental music.

His percussion ensemble conveys an entirely modern, urban and mechanistic sound world. Nothing was further from Varèse's thinking than the writing of some kind of neoprimitive, back-to-the-ancestral-pagan-past music, or than the writing of music that attempted to bridge the Orient with the West. His music is set in the midst of this century and in it we find, in quintessential form, the horror as well as poetry of modern urban life.

Electronic instruments began to appear slowly during the 1920s and 1930s. The most influential makers and pioneers were the Russian-born Leon Theremin (1896–1993) who invented the thereminvox or theremin, and the French-born Maurice Martenot (1898–1980) who invented the ondes martenots. Varèse was make use of them in *Equatorial* (1933–1934), scored for bass voice, four trumpets, four trombones, piano, organ, percussion and two theremins. In the revised version of 1961, the bass voice was augmented to two bass voices in unison and the theremins were changed to ondes martenots. *Equatorial* is a setting of a Spanish rendering of a Mayan prayer by the Guatemalan poet Miguel Angel Asturias. The composer's own view was that the time had arrived for these new electronic instruments to come to the fore, as he strongly believed that they would bring about a liberation from the tempered scale and also from ". . . the limitation of musical instruments". Electronic instruments were in his eyes paving the way ". . . towards the liberation of music".

In spite of these views, Varèse nevertheless wrote a short piece for solo flute, *Density 21.5* (1936). The title refers to the density of platinum, from which the new flute of the dedicatee George Barrere was made. Its 61 bars are a virtuoso exploration of the whole range of the flute. The exotic melody is akin to Debussy's *Syrinx* and *Canope*. But whereas Debussy's two pieces are poetic evocations, Varèse's *Density 21.5* remains aloof and desolate. Varèse has even added a new technique to the flute player's repertoire, by indicating that the player should strike the keys with his fingers instead of depressing them in the usual way.

From about 1936 to 1950 Varèse chose to be silent as a composer.

He felt discouraged and at times even embittered. The Second World War compounded his difficulties. Yet Varèse was lucky enough not only to witness his vindication but also to make a comeback as a composer of electronic music, placing him again in the vanguard of modern musical developments during the 1950s. The main impetus was given by the rapid development of electronic music after the Second World War and in the late 1940s Varèse became acquainted with the ideas of a French composer, Pierre Schaffer (born 1910) who was the creator of what was to become known as 'music concrete'. This is a technique in which the composition is worked out on disc or tape and in which the recording of any natural sound is reworked by, for example, changing speeds, playing in reverse and so on. The term eventually became used in the context of electronically-produced sounds as well, especially when the natural and artificial sound sources are combined.

In *Deserts* (1950–1954) Varèse was the first composer to combine an instrumental ensemble with tape. The instrumental section is scored for flutes, clarinets, horns, trumpets, trombones, tuba, piano and an assortment of percussion instruments played by five players. The electronic section consists of two magnetic two-track tapes on which electronically organised sounds are pre-recorded. They appear three times during the composition by means of the most delicate transition from orchestral sonorities to tape and vice versa, but never together. The composer explained that the first and third interpolations are "based on industrial sounds . . .", while the second ". . . is for an ensemble of percussive instruments". In describing the work, Varèse wrote:

> *Deserts* means to me not only the physical deserts of sand, sea, mountain, and snow, of outer space, of empty city streets; not only those stripped aspects of nature that suggest barrenness, aloofness, timelessness, but also that remote inner space no telescope can reach, where man is alone in a world of mystery and essential loneliness.[11]

This extraordinary composition, based on an ascetic reduction of thematic material, was first performed in 1954, in Paris, programmed between Mozart and Tchaikovsky! The scandal caused by this work was spectacular with shouts and angry protestations coming from the audience. But, of course, it was not the first time, nor will it be the last, that the public had been outraged by a new musical work, in Paris or anywhere else.

The apotheosis of Varèse's electronic vision of organised sound, with spatial music, was reached in 1958 with his *Poème électronique* (1957–1958). This composition was written in collaboration with the architect Le Corbusier, who designed the Philips Pavilion for the Brussels World Fair in 1958 where the music was to be played. Le Corbusier designed his pavilion, according to his own description, in the shape of the inside of a cow's stomach. The changing images exhibited in the pavilion were accompanied by continuous music but without any synchronisation between the visitors' visual impressions and the sounds. The composition was recorded on a three-track tape and the sound effects incorporated church bells in Brussels, industrial noises, jungle sounds, the passing of an aeroplane and the distorted screaming of a girl, among other elements. Varèse remarked that with his composition he ". . . wanted to express tragedy—and inquisition". In this eight-minute work, which was played continuously through some four hundred loudspeakers placed around the pavilion, he succeeded in expressing, largely by using noise, a poetic vision of our time in sound, in which nature, the fragments of organ music, chanting monks and the singing voice of a girl, are all submerged by the depersonalising forces of our technological age.

From 1961 to his death in 1965, he was preoccupied with *Nocturnal I* and *Nocturnal II (Nuit)* (the latter remaining unfinished), works based on Anaïs Nin's *The House of Incest*.

Out of his small number of compositions (less than a dozen) an even smaller selection of three works would be sufficient to reserve a place for him in the history of Western music. In *Ionization*, *Deserts* and *Poème électronique*, Varèse entered an uncharted world of sound which he alone knew how to navigate. Like Balzac's amazing musical hero, Gambara, he too could have said:

> Ma musique est belle, mais quand la musique passe de la sensation a l'idée, elle ne peut avoir que des gens de génie pour auditeurs,

car eux seuls ont la puissance de la développer. Mon malheur vient d'avoir écouté les concerts des anges et d'avoir cru que les hommes pouvaient les comprendre.

(My music is beautiful, but when the music passes from the sensa-tions to the idea, it can only have listeners of genius, because only they have the power to unfold it. My misfortune is to have listened to concerts given by angels and to have believed that people were able to comprehend them).[12]

8
Gambling with Sounds and Silence: John Cage

nothing is accomplished by writing a piece of music
nothing is accomplished by hearing a piece of music
nothing is accomplished by playing a piece of music
John Cage

JOHN CAGE (1912–1992) WAS BORN IN LOS ANGELES, California. His father was an inventor from Tennessee and it is fitting that this innovative composer has such a heritage—the desire to search and to experiment was, as it were, a family tradition. For his musical education, Cage studied both the piano and composition extensively and was a pupil of both Henry Cowell (1897–1965) and Arnold Schoenberg (1874–1951).

From his earliest composition, his desire to find a musical language without a personal insignia, or at any rate, to minimise the subjective in his composition as far as it was possible, was made apparent in his choice of free chromatic polyphony, a style in which he was largely influenced by Cowell, Schoenberg and Webern. This was soon followed by his adoption of the twelve-tone technique. In particular he felt an affinity with the idea of a thematic and non-harmonic compositional style and above all with the idea of thematic fragmentation and the increased use of silence. These procedures were largely absorbed from the musical style of Webern.

Cage's unusual lack of interest in harmony was noted by Schoenberg, who thought that his pupil's harmonic thinking was somewhat deficient. The unperturbed Cage found compensation in composing with very complex rhythmic patterns. His quasi-mathematically organised musical ideas, which involve both pitch and rhythm, are arranged in such a numeric way that the style of the composition is automated and almost completely depersonalised. His early compositions were already manifestations of this tendency for mechanical thinking. In these pieces he introduced the idea of using twenty-five pitches which appear without repetition in the framework of a very complex rhythmic counterpoint. The early example of the rhapsodic Sonata for Solo Clarinet (1933) indicates what was to gain fuller expression in the Sonata for Two Voices (1933) scored for any two or more instruments— note the free choice of instruments both in kind and number. These compositions were followed by *Solo with Obligato Accompaniment of Two Voices in Canon* (1933–1934). This also contains *Six Short Inventions*, based on the subject of the *Solo* for any three or more instruments. Both the canonic and invention writing enabled the composer to apply mechanical solutions which are predetermined by the *Solo*.

The use of the serial technique in Cage's works reached a climax in 1938 with three compositions. The first, *Metamorphoses for piano*, is a suite with five movements. The second, *Five Songs* for contralto and piano, consists of serial settings of E. E. Cummings's poems, including the playful text:

> in just—
> spring when the world is mud—
> luscious the little
> lame balloonman
> whistles far and near . . .

Here too, Cage is not unduly concerned about introducing a non-serial idea in the form of a chant-like drone. The third composition of the 1938 vintage is *Music for Wind Instruments* for flute, oboe, clarinet, horn and bassoon.

Two figures were even more influential on Cage than the members of the second Viennese school. These were Eric Satie, with his idea of 'furniture music' and 'non-intention', and Varèse, who also, as we have seen, was fascinated with noise and the possibilities of 'organised sound' leading to electronic music. These two composers were in turn influenced by the Dadaist and Futurist movements and above all by the Italian, Luigi Russolo (1885–1947), as Cage himself was to be.

As early as 1910, in one of the earliest Futurist manifestos,

Balilla Pratella (1880–1955) expressed his desire for a violent break with the past, that is, with traditional music. By 1912 he spoke vehemently in favour of atonality, the use of the quarter tone, irregular rhythm and so on. But even more radical was Russolo's own manifesto '*L'arti dei rumor*' of 1913, in which he advocated that music should not be based on notes of definite pitch, but on noises:

> . . . Today, music, as it becomes continually more complicated, strives to amalgamate the most dissonant, strange and harsh sounds. In this way we come even closer to noise-sound.[1]

His theory, which is a vindication of not so much 'the emancipation of dissonance', as Schoenberg put it, but rather of noise, was based on his view of the past which he believed had been relatively silent. It was during the nineteenth century when the real machine age came into being and the noise of machines was born and today, he goes on to say, "noise triumphs and reigns supreme over the sensibility of men".

These varied influences, whether coming from Webern or Russolo, had a profound effect on Cage's musical thinking. His compositions from the late 1930s onwards show a clear gravitation towards percussion music in which, naturally enough, rhythm dominates and in which silence gains a significant place. He saw a kinship between his approach to percussion music and to atonal music—that is, no sound is more important than another and silence is as integral a part of music as sound itself.

It was in Seattle, Washington, as a member of staff at the Cornish School, that Cage had the chance not only to experiment with but also to give concerts of percussion music. The fruits of these were *Imaginary Landscape no. 1* (1939), for percussive quartet with gramophones, and *First Construction (in Metal)* for percussion sextet, composed in the same year. In *Imaginary Landscape no. 1*, Cage not only introduced the piano as a percussive instrument, but revived Henry Cowell's idea of directing the performer to play inside the piano and not on the keyboard. For this effect he introduced the indication 'string piano'. Since Beethoven's time the piano has been used increasingly for its percussive potential. Liszt, Stravinsky and

Bartók, among others, explored the possibilities in this field. Cage went a stage further by using the 'prepared piano', that is, a piano modified by the insertion of, among other things, screws, nuts and bolts, spoons and small metal plates between the strings, drastically altering the original sound. While the idea had already been proposed and tried by Cowell in the 1920s, it was Cage who took it further and put it into systematic use. The practical merit of the prepared piano is that one player is able to give the musical impact of a whole percussion ensemble. This instrument was first introduced in his *Bacchanale* (1940) written specifically for prepared piano. This work was originally written in musical form for the dancer Syvilla Fort and was the first in a series of dance scores in which the prepared piano played a prominent role.

His later encounter with the choreographer Merce Cunningham in the early 1940s led to a most fruitful collaboration. Cage wrote some of his arguably most interesting scores for dance—for example, his first collaboration with Cunningham, *Credo in Us* (1942) for percussion quartet with electronic devices. The 'electronic devices' refer to a gramophone and a radio. The new idea in this composition was the random use of the radio, allowing the performer to switch it on at any station and to any programme which happens to be on the air at the time of the performance. The sole restriction was that news programmes should be avoided. The gramophone is programmed to play something classical. All this, combined with a percussion ensemble, creates a strange impression even today. At first hearing, the general effect is, of course, anarchistic but all in all quite humorous—an aspect which is often (perhaps unintentionally) the saving grace of Cage's music, even when one may be for a time puzzled by some of his ideas. The humour is also a virtue largely overlooked in serious musicological discussion of Cage's music. Yet, the playfully innovative clowning of this *enfant terrible* is one of the endearing aspects of Cage's musical gestures. Not unlike Salvador Dalí, Cage has maintained an uncompromisingly frivolous posture, behind which lurks great originality and artistic integrity.

During the 1940s, several more Imaginary Landscapes and Constructions were created: *Second Construction* (1940) and *Third Construction* (1941) both for percussion quartet; *Imaginary Landscape no. 2* (1942) for percussion quintet with electric devices; *Imaginary Landscape no. 3* (1942) for percussion sextet with electric devices; and more settings of poems by E. E. Cummings—*Forever and Sunswell* (1942) and *Experiences no. 2* (1948), the latter utilising the music of *Experience no. 1* (1945) for two pianos. But even more important were his numerous compositions for prepared pianos in which he explored further the possibilities offered by his invention.

Cage moved to New York in 1942 and lived with artist friends such as the painter Max Ernst and the dancer Jean Erdman. During the 1940s and 1950s Cage wrote a large number of compositions for prepared piano in which his remarkable ear for timbre and texture gained full expression. For example, *She is Asleep* (1943) is a fascinating mixture of tom-tom music, wordless singing as well as prepared and unprepared piano sound effects. The first section of *She is Asleep* is a 'Quartet for twelve tom-toms'; the second section is for a 'Duet for voice and prepared piano'—the performer's singing is wordless; the third section entitled 'A Room', for piano or prepared piano, is perhaps the most revealing in the effects created using these different instruments. When it is played on the normal piano, its repeated notes are more reminiscent of Bartók's *Microkosmos* vol. VI, no. 142 than of Satie. But, when the same piece is played on the prepared piano, one enters, as if by magic, the world of the Orient and of the gamelan music of Bali.

It is appropriate at this point to discuss another major influence in Cage's creative evolution—his encounter with oriental music, encompassing Indonesia, India, China and Japan. The strange exoticism of Cage's music is pronounced, less because of his tongue-in-cheek *épater le bourgeois* attitude (reinforced by the precedents of Dada, Futurism, Satie, Schoenberg and Webern), than because his music barely adheres to the European classical musical tradition. None of the great masters of this century—Stravinsky, Bartók, Schoenberg, Webern—had even contemplated breaking away from the European musical tradition. Cage did, and largely discarded harmony, one of the glories of Western music. The classical musical instruments of orchestral and chamber music he either rejected or drastically modified. He mostly ignored traditional forms. He substituted the Renaissance idea of genius, with its subjective projection of the great personality making profound utterances, with his attempt to depersonalise music. By and large, his music sounds more oriental than western. One of Bartók's musical aims was to bridge the Orient with the West, but within the framework of Western musical tradition—a tradition which he moulded according to his vision but which he nevertheless cherished to the end of his life. Cage, on the other hand, sensing its end, turned to the Orient as a convert who found in oriental thought and music a style that is still potent as its premise is different (i.e. rhythmic, rather than harmonic), but above all, that is not worn out by the relentless pursuit of the new, as in the West.

And the Earth Shall Bear Again (1942) and *Totem Ancestor* (1943), both for prepared piano, were written for two American dancers, Valerie Bettis and Merce Cunningham respectively. This vigorous music, apart from its Balinesian sound effects, is nevertheless related to Western music in a similar way as say Bartók's *Allegro Barbaro* (1911) or 'From the Island of Bali' (*Microkosmos* vol. 14, no. 109). All of these represent neo-primitive musical utterances in Western music. In *A Book of Music* (1944) for two prepared pianos, he developed further his imaginative skill in writing for this newly-invented medium. He also paid homage to his friend, the French artist Marcel Duchamp, in the same manner, in *Music for Marcel Duchamp* (1947). Duchamp had been living in New York since 1915. His work had been influenced originally by Cubism and Futurism, but he became one of the leading figures of American Dada and a significant influence on Cage's thinking. Marcel Duchamp made himself notorious by exhibiting works of art which were based on ready-made objects, one of the best-known being the urinal. In *Music for Marcel Duchamp*, Cage's orientally-inspired rhythmic patterns are also in evidence, as it is playfully structured on the quasi-symmetrical balancing of the uneven number 11, which is reached by the combination 2+1+1+3+1+2+1.

It was Cage's preoccupation with Indian music and philosophy which found expression in the music which he composed during the late 1940s. He was particularly attracted to the Indian concept of the nine permanent emotions—heroic, erotic, wondrous, joyful, painful, fearful, angry, odious—all gravitating towards the ultimate state of inner tranquillity— combined with the Indian rhythmic cycles, the system of talas. His Sonatas are all meticulously worked out and notated to mathematical precision. At this time Cage was still preoccupied with the composition of music through rational means and, above all, with the desire to control sounds. His earlier preoccupation with numbers in connection with his chromatic free atonal style, followed by his adoption of serialism, was therefore still current in the late 1940s and was rigorously applied, as the following analysis of the rhythm of the Sonata no. 5 indicates:

> The piece is in a simple AB form. The A section is 18 measures long, the B 22.5, giving a ratio between the two section of 4:5. The 18 measures of A divide in half, 9+9, the 22.5 measures of B are divided 9+9+4.5. Each of the four 9-measure segments of both A and B is further sub-divided into 4+5 measures, a reflection at a lower level of the 4:5 ratio of the two large sections. At an even lower level, both the 4-measures and the 5-measure segments are divided in half, giving within each 9-measure segment a division of 2+2+2.5+2.5. Since there are 2 beats to each measure, these smaller segments take up 4+4+5+5 beats, giving a 4:5 ratio at a third level. The final 4.5 bars are also constructed of 4+5 beats.[2]

1951 was a particularly significant year for Cage. He completed his Concerto for prepared piano and chamber orchestra (1950–1951), a major work from his considerable output and the notorious *Imaginary Landscape no. 4* for twelve radios (twenty-four players). The Concerto for prepared piano is in many ways a summation of his music up to that point, as it consists not only of Webern-like sound effects and a striking use of silence and gamelan sonorities, but also has a complex rhythmic structure and reflects his overall desire to depersonalise his music. It consists of three parts which are played without break. These should not be equated with the traditional three movements of the classical concerto. According to the composer's own description, he composed it by using a series of charts on which the planning of the work took place. The rhythmic structure throughout the composition is based on the subdivision of 23, that is 3, 2, 4, 4, 2, 3, 5. In the third part of the Concerto where silence gains an accented prominence, five structured periods of silences are introduced. When working on his charts, Cage was for the first time confronted with the recognition that, while the traditional objective of music was to say something, it was also possible to say nothing. In the *Imaginary Landscape no. 4* (1951) the element of chance takes a lead role, as the work calls for twelve radios to be played by twenty-four players— twelve are in control of the dials for the wave lengths (the required wave lengths for each radio are indicated by the composer) and the other twelve performers are in control of the various dynamics on each radio. The random sound effect made by others are here co-ordinated into a cacophonous work of 'happenings'.

During the 1950s it became apparent that, under the influence of Eastern philosophy, in particular Zen Buddhism with its anti-rationalist teaching, Cage's desire to turn away from the Western concept of artistic tradition, individual taste and even memory, was an increasingly powerful force in his thinking. Above all, the reading and close study at Columbia University of the *I Ching*, the Chinese book of changes, turned him even further away from the Western concept of art. This classical work attributed to Wen Wang, who lived in the twelfth century BC, is a fascinating book on divination and gave Cage the idea of composing by chance. His four-volume long piano composition, *Music of Changes* (1951), was composed by using charts largely derived from the *I Ching* and so composed by the tossing of three coins, one of the means by which the *I Ching* was consulted. Thus what used to be the composer's own volition, that is the control of pitch, duration and timbre, are, with this new method, entirely left to chance. Hence the name 'chance music', or to use its Latin root, 'aleatoric music'. Since the early 1950s the element of chance remained one of the most important philosophical and compositional ingredients in Cage's musical thinking.

Silence gained further impetus in such works as *Waiting* (1952) for piano. In this short composition, the composer calls for 98 seconds of silence at the beginning of the piece and eighteen seconds of silence to conclude it. Perhaps one of his most extreme pieces of clowning, however, is a work where he entirely abdicates responsibility as a composer apart from indicating its duration, the notorious *4'33" for any instrument or ensemble* (1952). This work, which is usually performed by a so-called pianist who sits motionless and in complete silence in front of the piano for the duration of four minutes and 33 seconds, is the ultimate expression of Cage's belief that music is everything which sounds, whether it is the sound of an aeroplane, the buzzing of a fly, or of our own heart-beats. We should listen and become part of the world in a creative unity rather than seeking to dominate and shape it according to our desires. For a while all these innovations and oriental theories were received with bewilderment and ridicule. Yet many of his ideas turned out to be, both artistically and socially, prophetic as well as influential.

One could argue that Cage may have wished to expand his earlier exploration in the Concerto for prepared piano and chamber orchestra by composing another one, the Concerto for Piano and Orchestra (1957–1958). In this concerto the pianist has at his disposal eighty-four choices of compositions from which he is free to choose. He not only plays the piano, but also manipulates it by plucking the strings inside the piano. He even goes under the piano to hit it from below and is in charge of electronic instruments. As the material given to the players of the orchestra can also be freely selected by them, each performance is likely to be different both in sound and in duration. Togetherness is not the aim of the work and so the musicians are separated from each other as much as is practically possible.

Cage decided to follow up the shock effect of his 4'33" by 'composing' another in kind, *4'33" no. 2* or *0'0" for solo to be performed in any way by anyone* (1962). This indication speaks for itself. So do the first four of his numerous *Variations*. For example, *Variation I* for any number of players, any sound producing means (1958) and *Variation II* (1961), in which the performers are not only left to choose their own sounds, but are also free to improvise whenever they feel like it. Microphones are also used by the participants in order to take up the sounds of their own coughing and breathing. From silence and the quietest sound effects to the most harshly amplified dynamics, all are put into force in these compositions in which, in spite of all the chances and freedom given to the performers, a careful planning is evident. One of the paradoxes of Cage's compositional ideology and methods is that a great deal of thought and preparation were actually put into most of his works in order to achieve the unpredictable and his obsessive attempts at depersonalising his art. Despite all of these efforts, however, the personal touch of this musical inventor and clownish heretic is nevertheless obvious. After all, as a creative artist he can hardly deny himself. Despite his interest in Oriental philosophy and thought, Cage's monumental ego and spirit of adventure did not change. Apart from being a significant composer he was one of this century's great musical adventurers.

His next journey, on which he had already embarked in *Imaginary Landscape no. 1* in 1939, was his increasing interest in electronic music and its combination with chance. *Reunion* (1968), for example, used the ingenious idea of using an electrified chessboard in which the players' moves on the chessboard are translated into sound. Neo-Dadaist or 'action music', analogous to 'action painting' ideas were introduced into other more out of the way compositions. In one notorious example, in *Variation V, thirty-seven remarks re an audio-visual performance* (1965), he devised the idea of the performer cycling freely on a large array of electronic transmitters to produce sounds transmitted to a bewildered audience via a series of loudspeakers. It would be most unjust if Cage were to be remembered only for these artistic tomfooleries of the 1960s, or indeed, if his unfortunate flirtation with Mao's China during the 1970s was to be seen as more than simply an ill-thought out and ill-informed political flippancy, common enough among intellectuals.

Anarchists (and Cage saw himself as one) do have the unfortunate tendency to be lured into totalitarian traps in spite of their high-floating ideas concerning civil disobedience and the abolition of power and so on.

The transcendentalist writers, especially Henry David Thoreau, who made such an impact on Ives's thinking, also affected Cage's thinking during the 1970s. In Thoreau's writings the deep-rooted romantic American preoccupation, the return to nature, exemplified by his intuitive book *Walden* (1854), took shape. The Rousseauesque 'if only we could be in tune with nature, all would be well' longing for a primitive and innocent bond with nature is an idea that must have struck home in Cage's mind. An interesting experiment in listening to the sounds of nature were his scores based on the amplification of the sounds made by plants, as in *Child of Tree* (1975) and *Branches* (1976). Perhaps even more so, Thoreau's essay 'Civil Disobedience' of 1846, written in the defiant spirit of the Abolitionist movement and triggered by his refusal to pay taxes that were to finance pro-slavery war, must have also appealed to Cage.

In the massive setting of the two *Song Books* (1970), several texts from diverse sources are incorporated: Cage's own writings from *Empty Words* (1973–1978), passages from books on mushrooms (mycology was one of his many hobbies), extracts from newspapers, fragments of other languages, are all intermingled with passages from Thoreau's diaries and from 'Civil Disobedience'. The overall sound effects are remarkable and the work succeeds in musico-dramatic terms, unlike Copland who, in *Lincoln Portrait* for speaker and orchestra of 1942, with its broadly similar idea of using a famous American's writings, only managed to produce a trite propaganda piece. In the Preface to the two *Song Books*, Cage stated:

> The solos may be sung with or without other indeterminate music ... The solos may be used by one or more singers. Any number of solos in any order and any superimposition may be used. Superimposition is sometimes possible, since some are not songs, but are directives for theatrical activity (which, on the other hand, may include voice production). Given a total performance time-

length, each singer may make a program that will fill it. Given two or more singers, each should make an independent program, not fitted or related in a predetermined way to anyone else's program. Any resultant silence in a program is not to be feared.

It is significant that during the 1970s, apart from the *Song Books*, more works were composed with Thoreau in mind, for example *Mureau, mix from Thoreau's writings* (1972) and the fascinating *Score* (1974), which is a musical transcription of 40 drawings taken from the pages of Thoreau's diaries. A similarly graphic treatment was given to the *17 Drawings by Thoreau* (1978). To the long list of formative influences and pre-occupations—Dada, Futurism, Satie, Schoenberg, Webern, Duchamp, the Orient in general and *I Ching* in particular, Mao—the transcendentalist Thoreau must be added. Indeed, as Cage put it, when writing about his *Song Books*, ". . . we connect Satie with Thoreau".

Perhaps Cage, in his old age, turned to retrospection and, after decades professing the suppression of memory, past and tradition, went in search of his ancestry. The Thoreau-based works, together with his *Letters to Eric Satie* for voice and tape (1978) and his fascination with Joyce in *Roaratorio, an Irish Circus on Finnegan's Wake* of 1979 (an electronic composition incorporating the vast numbers of sounds referred to in the novel) indicate that this was so. Maybe against his own will, he became an establishment figure, with honours offered to him from all over the world, one of the most prestigious being the French Commandeur de l'Ordre des Arts et des Lettres. The once revolutionary anarchist also became a member of the American Academy of Arts and Sciences (in 1978).

In the 1980s, Cage did not surprise us with any new directions in his work. Instead he gave us some more vintage works in his now familiar style, such as *30 Pieces for 5 Orchestras* (1981) and its chamber counterpart *30 Pieces for String Quartet* (1983). Towards the end of his career, he showed a tendency to use instruments in a relatively conventional manner, yet with Cage the unexpected was always present. Anyone who wishes to gain a better understanding of his thinking would be advised to turn to his revealing essays, manifestos and other writings about his philosophy and *ars poetica*. The most important of these is the collection of essays and lectures *Silence* (1961). Further collections of his writings appeared *A Year from Monday* (1967) and *Themes and Variations* (1982). These books are provocative, often baffling, sometimes muddled and almost always infuriatingly mannered, but without exception they contain stimulating materials and offer an indispensable insight into one of our century's great musical inventors and irreverent *enfants terribles*.

9
Some Modernist Front-Runners:
Henry Cowell, Roger Sessions, Harry Partch, Elliott Carter, Milton Babbitt, Earle Brown and George Crumb

When a work of art appears to be in advance of its period, it is really the period that has lagged behind the work of art
Jean Cocteau

A CHARACTERISTICALLY AMERICAN MUSICAL profile has emerged from the chapters so far which can be summarised as a tendency to be in the vanguard of things modern and to have a real zest for the new. It is worth remembering that of the composers featured so far, several are notable for their striking originality, among them three who made innovatory contributions to the history of Western music, namely Ives, Varèse and Cage. There seems to be an American tradition of musical front-runners since Ives's time, maintaining an unbroken line of musical progressives to the present. In this chapter a brief introduction is offered to each of those composers who, in one way or another and with varying degrees of significance, represent a continuation of the American musical vanguard.

Henry Cowell (1897–1965)

The Californian-born Henry Cowell was of Irish descent. His parents were liberal thinkers in matters of education, believing in absolute freedom of choice. Consequently their son missed normal schooling beyond elementary level. His secondary education was provided by his mother while his musical education was largely self-taught, apart from a few years of violin instruction which he received as a small boy. From money he earned while in his teens by cultivating and selling plants, he bought himself a piano on which he soon learned to play and experiment as a composer. This brief biographical information is of interest because it reveals a characteristic feature of Cowell—his independent, self-made approach to life and art.

In his late 'teens he enrolled, however, for a more formal study of music at the University of California, Berkeley, under the guidance of Charles Seeger (1886–1979), a pioneering musicologist. He also studied, for one term, at the Institute of Musical Art in New York and for a while at Stanford University. But his independent talent was already manifesting itself. During 1916–19, while the other students were doing their academic exercises, he was working on a theoretical book *New Musical Resources*. Published in 1930, it is a highly original and stimulating treatise, in spite of the obvious influence of Seeger. It sets out to explain the important role of the overtone series in music, how it affects the totality of a composition and once this is recognised, how it can be fruitfully applied in modern musical thinking. Such ideas as 'dissonant counterpoint', a term introduced by Seeger, polyharmony, atonality and Cowell's famous and independently evolved 'tone-clusters' (although Ives had already used them), as well as rhythm, can all be related to the overtone system and were vindicated in this remarkable book.

With this type of theoretical and practical commitment, Cowell set out to defend the cause of modern music in general and contemporary American music in particular. He was the founder of the New Music Society in Los Angeles in 1925, as well as of a quarterly magazine on modern music, *New Music*, in 1927. He was among the first to champion Ives whose music he promoted with great perception in a now classic work of his written in collaboration with his wife, *Charles Ives and His Music* (1955). He was an indefatigable musicologist, writer, publisher, teacher and lecturer, as well as being a selfless defender of other composers' works. But he was, above all, a many-sided composer in whose works many interesting ideas are to be found. During the 1920s he made himself notorious by giving recitals in which he bewildered his unsuspecting audiences by playing the piano with both elbows and fists, as well as submerging himself under the piano lid in order to create unheard of sonorities on the strings.

As a composer his aim was to synthesise music from diverse cultures into a universal style. Thus the rich musical traditions of Europe, America, the Middle and Far East, and particularly of Ireland, were to be moulded into a pan-cultural music. Of his vast output, many of his works reflect an almost mystic intensity in his attempt to achieve this aim. Although some of the movements were withdrawn by the composer, the titles given to the seven movements of *American Melting Pot* (1940) for chamber orchestra are telling: Chorale (Teutonic-American), Air (Afro-American), Satire (Franco-American), Alapna (Oriental-American), Slavic Dance (Slavic-American), Rhumba (Latino-American) and Square Dance (Celtic-American).

Other works provide ample examples illustrating his universalist ambitions: Symphony no. 3 *Gaelic* (1942); Symphony no. 13 *Madras* (1956–1958) influenced by Indian music; Symphony no. 16 *Icelandic* (1962); Symphony no. 19 (1965) incorporating Indonesian effects; the two Japanese koto concertos, Concerto for Koto and Orchestra (1961–1962) and Concerto no. 2 for Koto and Orchestra in the form of a symphony (1964); and finally his *Concerto Grosso* (1963) in five movements, four of them based on music from different continents brought together in the last movement.

His particular and sustained interest in Irish music and Irish subject matter in many of his compositions was due partly to his Irish background and Irish friends, but more especially to his close association with the poet John Varian, who introduced him to legends and tales of Ireland. This Irishness in his music can be found in works, from his early *The Tides of Manaurnaum* (1917) for piano, which later reappeared in *Four Irish Tales* (1940) for piano and orchestra, to his folk-song arrangements of the 1940s, 'The Irish Girl' for chorus and piano (1945), 'Lilting Fancy (Nickelty-Nockelty)' for chorus (1949). Even in compositions which are not necessarily programmatic, he used Irish jigs, hornpipes and airs in both his chamber and orchestral music. Perhaps the most striking feature of Cowell's music manifested itself in his pioneering and even eccentric, manipulation of sound. In this he can be seen as an influential link between Ives and Cage. While John Cage was still a child, Cowell was exploring new sonic possibilities in works for the piano, such as *The Tides of Manaunaum* (1917) and *The Banshee* (1925) to both of which he applied 'tone-clusters' or 'massed seconds' and the 'string piano' technique . He even worked on the idea of chance in music which he called 'elastic form'. The idea of giving creative freedom to the performers by allowing them to choose parts of a composition (ie. pitch, rhythm, sections and movements and so forth) at random, was introduced as early as 1917 in his *Quartet Romantic* (1917). During the 1930s he wrote several compositions in this style, such as his String Quartet no. 3 (1935), nicknamed the 'Mozaic Quartet', because the musical structure, formed by random selection of the available movements, resembles a mosaic pattern.

During the 1940s however, Cowell turned to more moderate directions and his music became more tonality-orientated in an attempt to consolidate his diverse musical thoughts. This tendency was further enhanced by his renewed interest in American hymnology and folk music. The result was a most attractive series of compositions under the title *Hymn and Fuguing Tune for Various Instruments*. The diverse settings of these compositions were spread over two decades, from 1944 almost until his death. Nevertheless, shortly before he died, in his composition *26 Simultaneous Mosaics* (1963) for five players, he again returned to the idea of 'elastic form', which, in this case is made by the five players—clarinet, violin, cello, piano and percussion—playing a random selection of sections.

In addition to his work as a composer, he was also an influential teacher, numbering among his pupils Gershwin and Cage. As a composer Cowell was indebted to his friend Ives and in turn was a major influence on Cage. Without diminishing Cage's achievement and originality, it is fair to say that he stands on the shoulders of his teacher, who, like himself, was one of America's visionary pioneers.

Roger Sessions (1896–1985)

Roger Sessions was born in Brooklyn, New York. Like Walter Piston, he too was an academic who spent a considerable amount of his life teaching and writing in several institutions including Smith College and the Cleveland Institute of Music. After travelling in Europe between 1926 and 1933, he taught at Boston University in the 1930s, twice at Princeton University (1935–1945 and 1953–1965) and at the University of California, Berkeley (1945–1951). He was also the Norton Professor at Harvard during the late 1960s as well as a member of the Juilliard School. During his long and distinguished life he could count among his friends Aaron Copland, the two Italian composers Alfredo Casella (1883 –1947) and Luigi Dallapiccola (1904–1975), Paul Hindemith (1895–1963) and the conductor Otto Klemperer.

Ernest Bloch (1880–1959), a late romantic composer of Swiss/ American origin who later turned to Neo-classicism, exerted a lasting influence on Sessions from the time he was a young composer. Sessions was a traditionalist by temperament and philosophy, with his heart and mind deeply rooted in the German romantic musical style. Although he was markedly influenced by Stravinsky and the neo-classical musical development which came about at the end of World War I with such works as Prokofiev's *Classical Symphony* and Stravinsky's *Pulcinella*, his own style was forged by a romantic approach towards free atonal chromaticism. During the early 1950s, this was further moulded by his absorption of the serial technique, following Schoenberg's romantic expressionism rather than Webern's ascetic style. It is of interest to note that the conversion of both Stravinsky and Sessions to the 12 note camp took place after Schoenberg's death in 1951. It is also revealing that Stravinsky, as opposed to Sessions, was both temperamentally and intellectually more disposed to follow Webern's pioneering direction rather than the romantically oriented style of Schoenberg's serial thinking.

Sessions's style is not easy to absorb as it is dense, dissonant, powerful and serious. Attempts at classifying artists are not, at best, made in order to force them into convenient didactic boxes, but rather are an effort towards defining their styles for the benefit of the listener. It is in this spirit that Sessions's music may be classified as neo-romantic/expressionist. Another characteristic of his work was that, unlike his friend Copland, he did not care for the idea of making his music deliberately American. He believed that a national style had to come from the composer's own spirit as reflected in the music rather than through an ideological selection of nationalistic subject matters. For him, the question was, as he so eloquently stated in his essay 'Music in a Business Economy' from 1948:

> . . . Do we really want the decisive or the final characteristic of our music to be its local color, its tricks of so-called 'native' style—or are we not rather to strive first of all for genuine expression and let our musical culture develop naturally out of the impulses of gifted men who feel within themselves the strength to be really free and to build their music out of the elements that best suit them? [1]

In the same essay he also expressed, in a defensive tone, his disquiet concerning the tendency towards making music easy for the listener:

> . . . [the] erection of 'accessibility' or 'audience appeal' into a kind of dogma—'down with all that is (to use the terms adopted as battle cries) obscure, esoteric, difficult'—let us have only music of 'social significance' for the public; away with 'sterile individualism'. 'Music must appeal to the average listener, not to small groups; the composer must write for "humanity as a whole", not for himself and his friends and colleagues. [2]

The overall output of his long creative life is relatively modest, but the range of his compositions covers most major musical forms, from chamber music to opera, written in the manner of a perfectionist. His first major work was the First Symphony (1926–1927), written in a neo-classical style with definite tonal gravitations for each of its three movements: E minor, C major and E major. This was followed by the Piano Sonata no. 1 (1930) and then the fiendishly difficult Violin Concerto (1935) where the tonality (B minor) is vindicated through uncompromising discords. An unusual aspect of its orchestration is Sessions's decision to leave out the violins altogether from the orchestra, no doubt in order to give even more prominence to the solo violinist. The overall effect is, as a result, severe. His two string quartets, of which the first was composed in 1936 and the second in 1951, are somewhat Ivesian in their density.

Perhaps his most popular work, although that adjective is rather a misnomer in Sessions's case, is his Symphony no. 2 of 1947. Its style showed an increasing gravitation towards the Schoenbergian school, above all the work of Alban Berg (1885–1935), whose intricate blend of expressionist lyricism in both free atonal and serial style Sessions found congenial. The consistent chromaticism of this work makes the given key-signatures rather symbolic, although one could argue, as Wilfred Mellers does:

> . . . this Symphony starts from traditional values and a European idiom, it in effect inverts those values. Tonality becomes a negative, associated with the most virulently arrestive, even cruel music; a-tonality becomes a positive, in that it is associated with a search for tenderness and compassion, if not serenity, within the inner life.[3]

Sessions's first one act opera *The Trial of Lucullus* (1947) is based on the text of Bertold's anti-fascist play of 1939. But his most ambitious operatic work was his largely serial three-act *Montezuma* (1964) on which he had worked since 1947. The opera is about the tragic fate of the Aztec emperor Montezuma, who, in spite of his willingness to co-operate with the Spanish conquistadors headed by Cortez, is massacred with his people. The orchestra is of Wagnerian proportion, but the music itself is closer to Verdi, although the French grand opera style must have exerted its influence as well. A stylish idea is the near static staging of a pagan world with its high priests. In *Montezuma*, Sessions gave the American answer to the grand tradition of operatic writing. With its freely adopted serial language, it stands between Berg's operas and Schoenberg's *Moses und Aaron*. It is not only his masterpiece but also a masterpiece of the opera repertoire.

During the last two decades of his life he worked with res-
olute spirit and renewed energy, bringing the number of his
symphonies up to eight. The last, Symphony no. 8 (1968), is
especially imposing with its grand outline, as is his Concerto
for Orchestra (1981) which is a solid, forceful work of valedic-
tory nobility and an astonishing achievement for a man of
eighty-five.

Of his modest output of choral music, the work most likely
to be remembered is his setting of Walt Whitman's poem
'When Lilacs Last in the Dooryard Bloom'd' (1964–1970), an
elegiac cantata for Lincoln.

As a writer on music, Sessions's books *The Musical Experience of Composer, Performer, Listener* (1950) and *Reflections on the
Musical Life in the United States* (1956) are most rewarding, but
of particular interest is the collection of his essays edited by
Edward T. Cone under the title *Roger Sessions on Music* (1979).
This book gives a fascinating insight into Sessions's way of
thinking.

He was not avant-garde in the experimentalist-inventor
sense of the term, although he was among the first to assimilate the serial method of Schoenberg and to recognise the
importance of the Second Viennese School. More important
was Sessions's own attitude towards his art and country. Here
was an American composer who did not feel parochial. He
wrote his music and carried on his professional life with the
dignity of a man who knew his value and who regarded both
European and American cultural traditions as his birth-right—
which indeed they were. This is the secret of his massive individual standing. He did not nurture 'Americanism' but rather
the noblest aspirations of the human spirit in America:

> For, after all, we are Americans not through a purely geographical
> accident, but through a profound faith in certain human princi-
> ples which were affirmed as the basis on which our nation was
> founded. [4]

He takes this further in the conclusion to his essay 'On the
American Future' (1940):

> Certainly we, too, will create a 'tradition' if civilization is saved
> and if we really wholeheartedly desire it. It will come, not through

cultural isolationism or consciously nurtured 'Americanism' but through men who, having listened to the music which sings within them, are willing to let themselves be guided by it, wherever it may lead them. Such music and only such music, will be truly and profoundly American.[5]

Sessions was and will remain a civilising force in American musical culture.

Harry Partch (1901–1974)

Like Cowell, Partch was a Californian. As a musician he was, as they say, 'a natural', self-taught and independent. He was totally absorbed in his own musical vision which had little to do with schools, issues, European musical tradition and the search for identity, national or otherwise. He did not even feel tempted by the educational siren Nadia Boulanger.

Instead, he set himself the task of creating a musical world based on a rejection of the 'even tempered' Western system and replacing it with a 'microtonal system' which has, in place of the twelve semitones in an octave, forty-three micro-notes to an octave. By rejecting the just-intonation system, he did not break entirely new ground, as existing Oriental practice and theories support his ideas. Be that as it may, here was a composer who more or less rejected Western musical tradition and who put into practice, in California, a largely Oriental way of musical thinking. Moreover, his view of music was physical and theatre-orientated and so his own works combined something of classical Greek drama and Japanese Noh plays, where acting, dancing, singing and instrumental music, together with a highly stylised staging, are all used to create a semi-ritualistic experience. Like so many twentieth-century composers, Partch was dissatisfied with conventional instruments, which were inadequate for his ideas. He therefore turned himself into an inventor and maker of new, mainly percussive instruments which were substantially influenced by Polynesian examples and ensured the sound effects he sought.

Partch was by temperament a vagabond, who both in life-style and philosophy anticipated the Beat Generation of the late 1950s, as well as similar movements in the 1960s. He lived largely on casual work and by performing his own music, but from his early forties he augmented his living by research grants and posts in various universities, including a Guggenheim award, which enabled him to realise the twenty or so new instruments he invented.

He dropped out, as he put it, 'intuitively' from the European/American instrumental and concert music tradition. He set out to create a largely monophonic based 'corporeal' theatre music founded upon the following elements, as he lists them in his book *Genesis of Music*:

> Stories sung or chanted, including folk music. Poems recited or intoned, including some folk music and some, but not all, popular music. Dramas, such as the early seventeenth-century Florentine music dramas, for example.
> Music intended specifically for dances which tell a story or describe a situation; both ancient and modern.[6]

In short, his music was to be based on harmonised spoken words, performed on new instruments and in an entirely new scale system.

His new instruments are visually highly decorative and as such, form part of the stage decor. The sounds of these instruments, for example his famous guard tree and cone gongs, resemble oriental percussive instruments. He also created a reed organ with a keyboard called 'chromelodeon' upon which the 43 micro-tones per octave are made playable. He has extended the marimba family with his own inventions (for example, the bass marimba and Marimba Eroica) as well as conventional instruments which he modified, like the viola and sitar.

Of his two dozen or so compositions (he destroyed his early works which he though to be too conventional), *US Highball: A Musical Account of a Transcontinental Hobo Trip* (1943) is as telling of the man as of his music. It is also a composition in which the chromelodeon is used. The composer himself gave the following programme note:

> The first part is a long and jerky passage by drags (slow freights) to Little America, Wyoming. The second is an adagio dishwashing

movement at Little America. The third is a rhythmic allegro, mostly by highway (hitch-hiking) to Chicago. The one word, Chicago, is the end of the text. Instrumentally, what follows implies a tremendous let down from the obstinately compulsive exhilaration of getting to Chicago. It implies bewilderment and that ever-dominant question in the life of the wanderer—what next?[7]

He was interested in Classical Greek mathematical and acoustical theories as they supported his own theories and he was equally fascinated by Greek dramas. Some of these he set to music, for example *Oedipus* (dance music after Sophocles) 1951, based on Yeats's version of the play by Sophocles, and the *Bacchae* of Euripides with the title *Revelation in the Courthouse Park* (1960).

It is interesting to note the choice of texts which impelled him to write music: Thomas Wolfe, Arthur Rimbaud, Lewis Carroll and James Joyce, whose *Finnegan's Wake* inspired him to write *Two Settings from Joyce's Finnegan's Wake: Isobel, Annah the Allmaziful* (1944) for soprano, kithara and two flutes.

There can be no doubt about Partch's integrity as a composer and inventor of visually and aurally fascinating and beautiful instruments. It is to the credit of the University of California and the various research and charitable foundations that he was supported by them. In his old age he became part of the Californian campus culture.

After his death in 1974, his valuable instruments were preserved in the care of the Harry Partch Foundation of San Diego, California. But, to quote a fellow American observer's view:

> Partch and his music lived on the fringes of the musical life of America. The fact that his music could be played only on instruments of his own design meant that none of his pieces was even performed by established musical organizations. His was an intensely personal and private music, inaccessible and unknown to most Americans.[8]

In an eccentric gesture, he seems to have barred his music from being performed. Should this remain the case, the loss will surely be ours for behind the hobo-like eccentricity (or perhaps because of it), his music-theatre bears witness to our time and America's cultural life.

Elliott Carter (born 1908)

The New York-born Carter turned to music via philosophy and English literature, subjects which he studied before becoming a pupil of Walter Piston at Harvard University and of Gustav Holst who was a visiting professor. Having graduated in 1932 in both literature and music, there followed the inevitable sojourn in France studying with Nadia Boulanger. After three years there, he returned to America in 1935 where he pursued a distinguished career as a composer, teacher, critic and leading advocate of contemporary music.

Out of his five years as music director with the American Ballet Caravan came the seldom-heard but distinguished ballet score *Pocahontas* (1939) based on the life of the legendary American Indian girl. His works written up to the 1940s, including his Symphony no. 1 (1942) and the *Holiday Overture* (1944), were influenced not only by Debussy, Stravinsky and by Ives, who had given him encouragement and support since he was sixteen, but also by Copland, whose Americanised neo-classicism Carter found congenial at that time.

During the post-war period his style evolved in an increasingly chromatic and dissonant way, in which aspects of the twelve-tone system were also absorbed but not adhered to dogmatically. Carter prefers to think in small units or 'cells' of three or four notes, which are then manipulated both horizontally (melody) and vertically (harmony). The transition from the neo-classical to the denser chromatic, quasi-atonal world began with his Piano Sonata (1946) although it still shows the influences of both Copland and Ives. An ingenious further development was his introduction of an intricate rhythmic organisation, referred to as 'metric modulation'. From the starting point of polyrhythm he evolved a system subtlely affecting the tempi of a composition by making it possible to pass (ie. modulate) rhythmically from one pulse to another. This is done by introducing a new beat in the original tempo thereby creating a new rhythm. For instance, in a duple time consisting of four quaver units, a set of quintuples are introduced and from that point, as Carter treats the notes of the quintuples as his new units, they take over from the old units of four, thus accelerating the tempo. When this technique is applied to several instruments, a string quartet for example, the linear independence of the players gives the sensation of several speeds playing at the same time.

Carter's neo-classical style, which he never abandoned, was further enriched by a highly individual approach to his art. After the Piano Sonata, the Sonata for Cello and Piano (1948), in which the idea of the 'metric modulation' was put into full effect, marks a further step towards his mature period. Having found his own voice, several outstanding compositions were created during and after the 1950s, notably of chamber music. His contribution to the string quartet repertory, especially String Quartet no. 1 (1951) and String Quartet no. 2 (1959), have been claimed to be worthy successors of Bartók's.

Carter's lifelong interest in literature and philosophy reveals itself in his illuminating programme note (1969) to his Sonata for Cello and Piano. In it, he not only tells us that the idea of 'metric modulation' came to him while composing this music, but that the basic idea of the work was to contrast the cello, representing 'psychological time' and the piano which in turn represents 'chronometric time'. When these are combined together they produce musical or 'virtual time'. The reference to virtual time reveals his indebtedness to the writings of Susanne K. Langer, one of America's most remarkable thinkers, whose books *Philosophy in a New Key: A Study in the Symbolism of Reason, Rite and Art* (1942) and its sequel *Feeling and Form: A Theory of Art* are among the most significant contributions to the study of art since Benedetto Croce. One of her statements concerning virtual time reads:

> . . . Musical duration is an image of what might be termed 'lived' or 'experienced' time—the passage of life that we feel as expectations become 'now' and 'now' turns into unalterable fact. Such passage is measurable only in terms of sensibilities, tensions and emotions; and it has not merely a different measure, but an altogether different structure from practical or scientific time.
>
> The semblance of this vital, experiential time is the primary illusion of music. All music creates an order of virtual time, in which its sonorous forms move in relation to each other—always and only

to each other, for nothing else exists there. Virtual time is as separate from the sequence of actual happenings as virtual space from
actual space.[9]

Carter reveals his intention even further when he concludes:

> The whole is one large motion in which all the parts are interre-
> lated in speed and often in idea; even the breaks between move-
> ments are slurred over. That is: at the end of the second
> movement, the piano predicts the notes and speed of the cello's
> opening of the third, while the cello's conclusion of the third pre-
> dicts in a similar way the piano's opening of the fourth and this
> movement concludes with a return to the beginning in a circulate
> way like Joyce's *Finnegan's Wake*.[10]

Likewise, String Quartet no. 1 has an extra-musical affiliation, this time with the general plan of Jean Cocteau's allegor-
ical film-fantasy *Le Sang d'un Poete* of 1930, which is concerned
with artistic creativity. The film starts with the blowing up of a
tall chimney. As it begins to fall apart the scene is stopped, only
to be returned to at the end of the film when the final collapse
is shown. The composer tells us:

> A similar interrupted continuity is employed in this quartet's
> starting with a cadenza for cello alone that is continued by the first
> violin alone at the very end. On one level, I interpret Cocteau's
> idea (and my own) as establishing the difference between external
> time (measured by the falling chimney, or the cadenza) and
> internal dream time (the main body of the work)—the dream time
> lasting but a moment of external time but from the dreamer's
> point of view, a long stretch.[11]

Carter goes on to say that his opening cadenza is an introduction to what is to follow and when it returns, it is placed at the
end of the composition as the final variation is a set of variations which constitutes the form of the finale. He adds:

> Not only is this plan like that of many 'circular' works of modern
> literature, but the interlocked presentation of ideas parallels many
> characteristic devices found in Joyce and others—the controlled
> 'steam of consciousness', the 'epiphany', the many uses of punctu-
> ation, of grammatical ambiguities, including the use of quotation.[12]

The latter is a reference to two quotations, one from the opening
of Ives's Violin Sonata no. 1, the other a rhythmic pattern taken

from Conlon Nancarrow's (born 1912) *First Rhythmic Study*. They are used in homage to the friendship and inspiring help of these two composers.

String Quartet no. 2 has won Carter three prestigious awards, the Pulitzer Prize in Music (1960), the New York Music Critics Award (1960) and the UNESCO First Prize—International Rostrum of Composers (1960). In the quartet's six continuous sections (Introduction, I. Allegro fantastico, II. Presto scherzando, III. Andante expressive, IV. Allegro, Conclusion), the concept of individualisation as applied to music is made emphatically obvious by giving each of the four instruments a characteristic melodic, harmonic and rhythmic profile that results "in four different patterns of slow and fast tempi with associated types of expression".[13] The overall effect is that the four players in this quartet are not so much playing together, but rather asserting their individualities in company.

Looking back to his String Quartet nos. 1 and 2 in a programme note for a record release written in 1970, Carter drew attention to the relationship between the two quartets by stressing that "The musical language of the Second Quartet emerged almost unconsciously through working during the '50s with ideas the First gave rise to."[14] Characteristically, after quoting a passage concerning time from Thomas Mann's *The Magic Mountain*, he proceeds with a pertinent statement, again backed by literary comparisons:

> Although both quartets are concerned with motion, change, progression in which literal or mechanical repetition finds little place, yet the development of musical expression and thought during the eight years that separate them seems to me far-reaching. The difference, aside from that of their time-scales, might be compared to the types of continuities found in Mann's own writings, where in the earlier ones, characters maintain their characterised identities with some revelatory changes throughout a work, while in the Joseph novels, each character is an examplification of an archetype whose various other incarnations are constantly referred to (as Joyce does in another way in *Finnegans Wake*).[15]

String Quartet no. 3 (1971), inspite of its conceptual brilliance and instrumental virtuosity, has not made the same impact as the first two quartets so far.

During the 1950s and 1960s he also composed three major orchestral works, Variations for Orchestra (1954–1959), Double Concerto (1961) for harpsicord, piano and two chamber orchestras and Concerto for Orchestra (1969). The titles themselves indicate Carter's sustained neo-classical leanings, but the dense language continues to reveal the mind of a complex musical thinker who does not take tradition lightly. He set out to maintain a continuity between past and present and by moulding it in his own fashion, he succeeded in extending, in his best works, the boundaries of traditional style with new ideas. It is largely on this basis that Carter's importance as a contemporary composer stands.

The 1970s and the first half of the 1980s showed a preoccupation with complex handling of instrumental ensembles: *A Symphony of Three Orchestras* (1979) and the remarkable *Penthode* (1984–1985) for an ensemble of five instrumental quartets. *To Sleep, To Thunder* (1982), a setting of poems by Robert Lowell for tenor and chamber ensemble, added to the composer's modest, but fine contribution to vocal music.

Carter belongs to the American experimentalist tradition but it is his markedly synthesist approach to his art in which past and present developments gain new meanings—often with analogous references to contemporary literary trends—that gives his music its highly cultured imprint.

Milton Babbitt (born 1916)

Babbitt was born in Philadelphia into a family where mathematics was taken for granted, his father being an actuary. Although Babbitt studied both the violin and the clarinet and showed early signs of interest in composing music, he possessed an equally strong bent towards mathematics which he studied at the University of Pennsylvania from 1931. But, disillusioned with the method of teaching there at that time, he left to study music at New York University where he finally graduated in 1935. He also had the good fortune to be able to study privately for three years with Roger Sessions. It was Sessions who directed the young composer towards new possibilities in music and whose inspiring teaching made a deep impression. During the course of three years he familiarised himself with the works of Stravinsky and the members of the Second Viennese School and, as a result adopted the twelve-note compositional style.

In 1938, he became a member of the Music Faculty at Princeton, where he served for decades as a dedicated teacher and formidable exponent of the serial system. He never abandoned mathematics as a subject and in fact, during the Second World War, he taught in the Mathematics Department at Princeton. In music, he applied the logical rigour of mathematics to his own compositions. Characterised by a cerebral and procedural approach to music, his work has maintained this style throughout his career. It is enough to read the headings of his essays—'The Function of Set Structure in the Twelve-Tone System' (1946), 'Twelve-Tone Invariants as Compositional Determinants' (1960), 'Set Structure as a Compositional Determinant' (1961) and 'Twelve-Tone Rhythmic Structure and the Electronic Medium' (1962)—to realise his highly technical approach. The essays themselves make but very few references to art in the aesthetic, emotional sense of the term—on the contrary, they are avoided. Pitches, intervals, harmony and dynamics, which have been part of the emotional vocabulary of composers for centuries, are in Babbitt's method distilled, if not sterilised, into precise calculations expressed by numbers and meticulously worked out patterns. Nothing is left to chance, inspiration or instinct. Unlike Varèse, behind whose pseudo-scientific vocabulary so much fun and poetry lurk, Babbitt's work is truly technical. His music may at first leave many listeners cool, but repeated listening reveals an intellectual wit which has its own particular aesthetic satisfaction and strange beauty.

Babbitt's approach to music is rigidly founded on the premise that the twelve-tone set not only determines the pitch, but every other aspect of the music: harmony, rhythm, dynamics, timbre and so on. Once the twelve tones are selected, they dominate both the linear and the vertical aspects of the composition in the strictly fixed order in which the twelve-tone set has been composed. No deviation is allowed to occur. Any analogy with tonal music is not only avoided but made entirely irrelevant. Alban Berg's poetic lyricism is here entirely rejected in favour of a severely handled ascetic compositional technique in which the romantic notion of music 'from the heart to the heart' is replaced with music from the head to the head. Babbitt's attitude is entirely unambiguous. He is not seeking popularity, on the contrary, he takes his relative isolation from the public as an inevitable aspect of his work, as he is not concerned with the views, the likes or dislikes of the layman whose knowledge, if any, is likely to be limited. His music is primarily for the initiated, in the same way as an atomic physicist's calculations on a seminar room's blackboard are. This analogy is a fitting one, as much of America's musical activity in experimental and electronic music is taking place under the aegis of the universities.

The first compositions which gained the composer's approval for posterity were *Three Compositions* (1946–1947), for piano, and *Composition for Four Instruments* (1947) for flute, clarinet, violin and cello. These works show the influence of Schoenberg and Webern as well as Stravinsky while also being marked by Babbitt's predilections for logical manipulation of sound and the move towards 'total serialism'. The *Composition for Four Instruments* (also for flute, clarinet, violin and cello), as well as String Quartet no. 1, both from 1948, and String Quartet no. 2 (1954) reflect Webern's cerebral writing. An unusual commission by the Brandeis Festival of the Creative Arts in 1957 inspired him to compose for a jazz ensemble. The work is titled *All Set* (1957) and became notorious through Babbitt's application of the serial technique in combination with the characteristic elements of jazz.

With his interest in logic and composition, it was inevitable that during the 1950s Babbitt would gravitate towards electronic music. The idea of possessing total control over a strictly determined, mathematically calculated complex score was the very thing to which he aspired. During this period, he was invited to work as a composer-consultant on the Mark II RCA synthesiser at the Columbia-Princeton Center. Indeed, one can see in his first work for synthesiser, *Composition for Synthesiser* (1961), that the composer had found his element. Several more works followed in the 1960s and 1970s, including a setting of Dylan Thomas's 'Vision and Prayer' (1961) for soprano, synthesiser and 4-track tape. This has the unique distinction of being the first work in which a synthesiser is used to accompany a singer. *Ensembles for Synthesiser* (1962–1964) and *Occasional Variations* (1971) were written purely for four-track tape but Babbitt soon found that special sonorities can be obtained by combining conventional instruments with electronic sound effects. This resulted in a series of works in which this combination is ingeniously realised, for example, in Concerto for violin, small orchestra and tape (1974–1976), *Reflections for piano and tape* (1975) and *Images for saxophone and tape* (1979).

Of course the musical language of Babbitt remains firmly based on serial thinking. He adapted the twelve-tone technique to electronic music making. How much the composer was aware of the implication of his artistic and scientific search for expressing the new in sound is perhaps best illustrated by his early essay written in 1962 for the then new periodical *Perspective of New Music*. In his formidable article entitled 'Twelve-tone rhythmic structure and the electronic medium', he wrote:

> To proceed from an assertion of what music has been to an assertion of what music, therefore, must be, is to commit a familiar fallacy; to proceed from an assertion of the properties of the electronic medium to an assertion of what music produced by this medium therefore must be, is not only to commit the same fallacy (and thus do fallacies make strange bedfellows), but to misconstrue that compositional revolution of which the electronic medium has been the enabling instrument. For this revolution has effected, summarily and almost completely, a transfer of the limits of musical composition from the limits of the nonelectronic medium and the human performer, not to the limits of this most extensive and flexible of media but to those more restrictive, more intricate, far less well understood limits: the perceptual and conceptual capacities of the human auditor.[16]

In spite of his profound involvement with electronic media, Babbitt continued to write for conventional instruments and voices, including three more string quartets (two in 1970 and one in 1982), *A Solo Requiem* (1976–77) for soprano and two pianos and Concerto for Piano and Orchestra (1985).

Behind his self-confessed cerebral approach to music, which at times can be forbidding, a genuine artistic playfulness nevertheless shines through. This, on occasions, can give the pleasing impression of a Klee-like patternmaker in music, especially in those compositions where the electronic and the conventional instrument or human voice are combined. Babbitt is a craftsman of our scientifically orientated age and his music a testimony of its potential for artistic expression.

Earle Brown (born 1926)

A follower and member of the Cage circle, Brown belongs to the 'New York School' of the 1950s which included such gifted musicians as Morton Feldman (born 1926), David Tudor (born 1926) and Christian Wolfe (born 1934). Like Babbitt, Brown too is interested in mathematics, but unlike Babbitt, he qualified in engineering and mathematics before turning to music. Influenced by the theories of the Russian-American composer and mathematician Joseph Schillinger (1895–1943), whose book *The Mathematical Basis of Arts*, left a deep impression on him, he quickly established himself as a leading figure of the American avant-garde with his graphic notation and compositions largely based on 'controlled indeterminacy'.

In such works as *December* (1952), all resemblance to traditional notation is abandoned for a graphic notation which looks more like a painting by Mondrian. Needless to say, the performer is called upon to learn the meaning of the differently sized and positioned black lines on the canvas-like score, which is then 'realised' on sometimes unspecified instruments. The strong influence of visual art on Brown's musical thinking was stressed by the composer himself in connection with the recording of his *Hodograph 1* (1959) when he wrote:

> The earliest, strongest and still the predominant influence of my
> conceptual attitude toward art and 'poetics' were the works of

Alexander Calder and Jackson Pollock, which I remember seeing first in 1948 and 1949 and Max Ernst's book, *Beyond Painting*, which I read in 1950 and which was in a sense the verbal confirmation of what I felt in the Calder and Pollock works: the function of non-control and the 'finding' of aspects of the work within the process of 'making' the work.[17]

The twenty-five pages of the score for his piano composition titled *Twenty-five Pages* (1953) and *Available Forms I* (1961), perhaps his best-known composition, possess a quality which is reminiscent of the sculpture mobiles of the artist Alexander Calder (born 1898)—who, in fact, also started his career as an engineer before turning to art. Indeed, one of his unpublished compositions is called *Calder Piece* (1963–1966), for four percussionists and a Calder mobile where the instrumentalists relate to the movements of the sculpture as if it were a conductor—an unsual combination of two art forms. *Available Forms I* was written for a chamber orchestra of eighteen performers using the 'open form' technique which enables the performers to choose from any of the available six pages and any of the events contained on these pages. The listeners are thereby under the impression that they are witnessing the actual forming of the composition by the performers. The dichotomy of 'controlled chance' is solved by the composer offering his musical material to the performers who in turn utilise it according to their own wishes. They play a significant creative role—the performer is no longer just an executor of a composition, but a creative collaborator with the composer.

The Rome Radio Orchestra commissioned a large scale orchestral composition from him and his answer to the challenge was *Available Forms II* (1962) in which the same concept behind *Available Forms I* was used, but in an enlarged version involving the presence of two conductors.

From the mid-1960s onwards, Brown seems to have mellowed, tending towards compositions in which a compromise is reached between the aleatoric elements of 'open form' and the more conventional and thorough style of composing. Representative works from this period are the String Quartet (1965), *Modules I–III* (1966–1969) for orchestra, *Time Spans* (1972) for large orchestra and *Sounder Rounds* (1982) for orchestra.

Brown's contribution to the contemporary musical scene largely consists of his ingenious consolidation of ideas such as aleatory music which Cage initiated. And under the influence of Calder's sculpture, he translated into sound the mobile's simultaneous motion and stillness. This was a idea Eric Satie had already experimented with, especially in his piano music, but Brown developed it further and succeeded in adapting it to large-scale compositions, for example, in *Available Forms I* where the flute and clarinet play long pedal points, giving a sensation of motionlessness against which animation and dynamic forces are juxtaposed.

George Crumb (born 1929)

The work of George Crumb, the son of two professional musicians, came into prominence during the late 1960s and 1970s. His music is characterised by a poetic vision largely expressed in programmatic compositions in which a wide range of avant-garde techniques are used. The influence of Webern, the sound of Asiatic music, aleatory ideas and electronically-modified instruments are all to be found in his music. It is clear however that these tricks of the trade, as it were, are not part of a fanciful intellectual game or used to *épater le bourgeois* but are employed to create richly lyrical and dramatic works. For him music is meant to be an enriching and uplifting experience and it is no wonder that Béla Bartók's music features prominently among those who have influenced Crumb's musical thinking.

Reading the poetry of Federico Garcia Lorca inspired Crumb to set several of the poems. The intensity of Crumb's preoccupation with these works can be measured by the following impressive selection of his Lorca-inspired compositions: *Night Music I* (1963), *Songs, Drones and Refrains of Death* (1968), *Madrigals: Books III and IV* (1969), *Night of the Four Moons* (1969) and *Ancient Voices of Children* (1970).

Another significant feature of Crumb's style is his predeliction for musical quotation which may be taken from works by Bach, Schubert and so on. These quotations are treated by the composer not so much in order to integrate the old with the new, but rather as points at which the listener can relate to the music and feel reassured. As Richard Steinitz put it:

> The direct quotations from Bach, Schubert or Chopin, heard through Crumb's strange and unworldly soundscape, acquire an amazing aura of distance both cultural and temporal. Surrealist museum exhibits, their mummified beauty seems utterly remote, like a childhood memory of warm, homely security.[18]

Two compositions stand out among his works so far for their highly imaginative sound effects and lyrical poetry: *Ancient Voices of Children* for soprano and chamber ensemble, which includes a mandolin and a toy-piano, and the quartet called *Black Angels* (1970). In the notes written for and the recording of *Black Angels*, Crumb wrote:

> *Black Angels (Thirteen Images from the Dark Land)* was conceived as a kind of parable on our troubled contemporary world. The numerous quasi-programmatic allusions in the work are there-fore symbolic although the essential polarity—God versus Devil—implies more than a purely metaphysical reality. The image of the 'black angel' was a conventional device used by early painters to symbolize the fallen angel.

Accordingly, in its "huge arch-like design" as the composer put it, we are offered a spiritual journey, a "voyage of the soul" in which the fall from grace, spiritual annihilation and redemption are all given expression. For this effect the work is packed with traditional symbols such as the cabbalistic numbers of 7 and 13, *Diabolus in Musica* (the tritone—diminished fifth or augmented fourth), the 'Devil's trill', introduced to string music by the eighteenth-century Italian composer and violinist Guiseppe Tartini, together with quotations from the medieval chant 'Dies Irae' and Schubert's famous theme from 'Death and the Maiden'. The four string instruments are electronically amplified in order to heighten the surrealistic effects and the performers are also asked to play, from time to time, instruments other than the conventional two violins, viola and cello, such as maracas, tam-tams and three sets of water-tuned crystal glasses as well as counting ritualistically in several languages, including Hungarian and Swahili. All this may seem

gimmicky, but Crumb has the power to enchant us with mag-
nificent sonorities guided by his acute hearing and poetic
imagination in sound. It is by no means far-fetched to say that
what Messiaen's *Quator pour la fin du temps* was for the 1940s,
Crumb's *Black Angels* was for the 1970s.

Influenced by Bartók's set of didactic compositions,
Microkosmos and Cage's prepared piano music, Crumb has
added to the twentieth-century repertoire a significant series of
piano works under the general heading *Makrokosmos*. Each of
the four volumes has been given a programmatic title. The first
two volumes (1972 and 1973 respectively) are called *12 Fantasy
Pieces after the Zodiak*; the third volume, *Music for a Summer
Evening* (1974); and volume four *Celestial Mechanics* (1979).
These works, like *Gnomic Variations* (1981) and *Processional*
(1983) also for piano, invite us into Crumb's universe of sound.
His piano technique, which runs practically the whole gamut
of modern pianism, sounds as if it is written by an incorrigible
romantic. For this reason his music is among the most readily
accessible of the post-war avant-garde composers.

It is hoped that this chapter has impressed upon the reader not
only the rich variety of American musical talents, but also how
adventurous these composers are in their search for new
musical expressions. It is through their work that America in
the twentieth century has found its own voice. American music
is no longer influenced but rather has in its turn become an
influencing force in the contemporary musical scene.

10
The Minimalists:
La Monte Young, Terry Riley, Steve Reich, Philip Glass and John Adams

. . . stiff resistance to genuinely new ideas is more widespread than is generally acknowledged . . .
Philip Glass

INIMALISM IS A TERM WHICH CAME INTO currency during the 1960s, first, as so often in the history of musical terminology, in connection with the painting and sculpture of the time. One of the aims of American painters and sculptors was to reduce materials, structure and colour to their most basic or minimal elements. The American minimalist painters of the 1960s, such as Dan Flavin, Don Judd and Frank Stella, to mention only a few, could trace a distinguished ancestry back to Europe before the First World War as many of their views were anticipated and shared by the Russian suprematists headed by Kasimir Malevich, the constructivist Vladimir Tatlin, as well as by the dadaists. But whereas minimalism in art influenced 'pop art', it was 'pop music' which had some influence on minimalism in music, which will be referred to later.

In the sphere of music, the minimalists set out to reject the complexities of the largely serial thinking which dominated the post-Second World War period. They proposed instead a return to tonality and modality in their most elementary forms in which harmonic movements are reduced to the minimum and obstinate repetitions of rhythmic patterns and small diatonic melodic units are used. The music thus created is reduced to its most elemental forces, the effect of which is not unlike some trance-inducing Oriental music. Herein lies the immediacy of its appeal to audiences, but not so much to the musical establishment, which, by and large, equates complexity with value.

Early minimalist music of the 1960s and early 1970s underwent, not surprisingly, a development which was not unlike that of jazz: both forms of music entered the musical scene via the back door—jazz was practised in bars, night-clubs and bordellos and minimalist music established itself via private performances in unusual places like attics and in galleries as part of visual art exhibitions. Although all the major minimalist composers referred to in this chapter were conservatory and university educated, they shared a profound dissatisfaction with what they saw as the stifling ethos of these establishments and therefore, while also gravitating towards other art forms, they embraced jazz, pop music and the music of both Africa and the Orient. In these styles of music they found freedom and an immediacy which they could not find in the ivory-tower of serialist scholasticism which largely dominated that period.

La Monte Young (born 1935)

La Monte Young is generally considered to be the founder of minimalism in music. In his college and university years he showed a marked interest in jazz and played in jazz ensembles. His interest in Karlheinz Stockhausen's music and the Darmstadt summer school activities, which became the Mecca of modern music with its Internationale Ferienkurse fur Neue Music, was, however, overshadowed by his encounter with north Indian classical music. He mastered this music sufficiently well to be able to perform it with his teacher Pran Nath from 1970. The depth of his involvement with Indian music can be measured by his appointment in 1971 to the directorship of the Kirana Center for Indian Classical Music.

Influenced by the long drone sounds used in Indian music as well as the medieval parallel organum, Young evolved a minimalist compositional style expressing a mystical communion with eternity. The music is quasi-static, simple in its harmonic language and highly repetitive.

During the 1960s and 1970s many composer-performers felt that the best way to ensure that their own music was performed was to form their own ensembles. Young, apart from being influentially involved with the Fluxus movement in New York during the first half of the 1960s[1], founded his own ensemble which he characteristically named Theatre of Eternal Music. Out of this grew the idea of creating a totality of arts, reminiscent of Wagner and Scriabin, which was to be performed in Dream Houses. In many ways this minimalist cultural experience was a readily accessible psychedelic and *son et lumière* version of Bayreuth. No wonder that the most popular venues for the Dream Houses performances were art galleries and museums, where Young's wife, the painter and lighting artist Maria Zazeela, provided some of the visual effects.

In a sustained way Young has gone out of his way to bewilder his listener and consequently isolate himself, with his neo-dadaist works such as *Poem for Chairs, Tables, Benches, etc . . .* (1960) which he requires to be performed on any sound sources, *Pre-tortoise Dream Music* (1964) for chamber ensemble including two saxophones, and *The Tortoise, His Dreams and Journeys* (1964) for voices, various instruments and electric drones. The work was named ". . . in honour of an animal that has the Youngian virtues of longevity and slowness"[2] as Paul Griffiths had wittily put it. This composition had several 'realisations' to which fanciful titles were given, such as 'The Tortoise Droning Selected Pitches from the Holy Numbers for the Two Black Tigers the Green Tiger and the Hermit'. As the composer had eternity in mind (or at least a very long time), these realisations remain on-going activities. It should be remembered that the idea of imitating eternity in music has a long tradition. In the fourteenth century, for example, Guillaume de Machaut composed a theologically inspired work *Ma fin et mon comencement* for voices in infinite canon, thus asserting the Christian belief that 'One's end is one's beginning'.

Young's long-standing preoccupation with 'just intonation', as opposed to 'well-tempered intonation' generally in use since Bach's time, has involved him in a continual realisation of *The Well-tuned Piano*. He began work on this composition for prepared piano in 1964 and since then several realisations have appeared and more are still likely to emerge from this uncompromising and masterful dreamer of eternity.

Terry Riley (born 1935)

Terry Riley is a composer-pianist who graduated from University of California before going to Paris in 1963, where he worked in recording studios. There he evolved a compositional style based on the ostinato repetition of a melodic phrase over a constant rhythmic pulse, which became not only his trademark but also that of the whole minimalist movement.

His *Keyboard Studies* (1963) and the notorious *In C* (1964) for unspecified melodic instruments, are by now classics of minimalist music. *In C* demands that the players improvise freely on fifty-three melodic patterns repetitively over a constant rhythmic pulse. The improvisatory approach to composition dominates Riley's thinking, so much so that from 1964 onward, he abandoned notation altogether in favour of improvised composition which is taped during the act of performance.

Riley, like Young, has also been influenced by Indian music. He too became a pupil of Pran Nath in India, with whom he studied the art of performing ragas. But whereas Young pursued a contemplative Eastern mysticism, this influence on Riley comes across as more pragmatic. He is interested in combining Western and Indian musical instruments, with the additional help of a synthesizer, to create a synthesis of multi-cultural sounds. This he achieves to great effect in *The Medicine Wheel* (1983) in which one of the cornerstones of Western chamber music making, the string quartet, is combined with, among other things, the sitar and tabla.

Also like Young, Riley is also attracted to 'just intonation'. Whether they were both influenced by Harry Partch's eccentric works, it is difficult to tell. What is interesting, is that the preoccupation with 'just intonation' came about not only as part of the revival of 'authentic' performances of old music, but also as a legitimate part of contemporary compositional technique.

Steve Reich (born 1936)

A somewhat similar educational background to Young and Riley characterises Reich's emergence on to the contemporary musical scene. The pattern is roughly as follows: college and university education; encounter with Oriental music; rejection of serialism and traditional Western musical forms in favour of largely rhythm orientated, repetitive, trance-inducing experimental forms. At first, all artistic activities are part of the avant-garde fringe but in time lead to recognition and honours.

Reich graduated in philosophy at Cornell University in 1957 and pursued the study of music privately as well as at the Juilliard School and at Mills College. His interest in rhythm—he studied the drum in his teens—was enriched by his encounter with African and Balinese music, an encounter which inspired him to study further non-Western music-making. These studies led to his evolving a compositional style which is emphatically rhythm-orientated and in which the conventional melodic and harmonic ideas are entirely subordinated, if not altogether discarded, in favour of percussive, pulse dominated compositional procedures.

Perhaps the most characteristic technical aspect of Reich's musical thinking is his use of canon, which he prefers to call 'phasing' based as it is on a technical device of using two tape recorders, one out of phase with the other from a chosen point in the piece, the ensuing discrepancy producing a contrapuntal, canonic texture. The first of this type of composition was *It's Gonna Rain* (1965), of which the composer says in his notes

> . . . The voice belongs to a young black Pentecostal preacher who called himself Brother Walter. I recorded him along with the pigeons and traffic one Sunday afternoon in Union Square in downtown San Francisco. Later at home I started playing with tape loops of his voice and, by accident, discovered the process of letting two identical loops go gradually out of phase with each other.[3]

Starting with the preacher's voice, the work evolves through the intoxicated cantations of Afro-American preaching to the percussive repetition of words—which, superficially, may give the impression of a gramophone needle stuck in its groove, but the magic is in the 'phasing' and in the relentless pulse—leading to 'controlled chaos' in eight voices, which according to the composer ". . . may be appropriate to the subject matter—the end of the world".

It is a truism to say that a creative idea, whether or not it is discovered accidentally, must possess enough potential for further development for the artist to mould it into his or her own style. Reich, having found a new possibility for composing complex polyphonic works with the technique of 'phasing', proceeded to unfold the interesting potential of his accidental discovery, enhancing it with African and Balinese rhythms as well as phasing, that is, technically induced beats.

His next composition in the evolution of this style was *Come Out* (1966). Again the human voice—which is that of a Harlem boy, Daniel Hamm, describing a beating in a police station—serves as the foundation for this composition which is then worked out on tape. To begin with one hears the voice in unison reciting "Come out to show them . . .", but soon a gradual, hardly perceptible 'phasing' is introduced, inducing a throbbing beat. These eventually lead to a series of canons for two, four and eventually eight voices. The opening incantation thus evolves into an exhilarating performance, comparable to ritualistic drumming and dancing. But it is achieved without direct imitation of non-Western music. It reflects rather, Reich's absorption and skilful application of ideas and not the more usual spicing of Western music with Oriental exoticisms.

Piano Phase (1967) was originally conceived for tape recorder and piano where the 'phasing' technique was applied to a live performer and the tape. This was then changed to an entirely live music performance for two pianos, for which the music is carefully written out with clear indications where and when the gradual phasing should start or come back again to the opening unison. Melodically, the music is based on the simplest (i.e., minimalist) means, which is then relentlessly repeated creating a mesmerising sensation from the constant oscillations.

An entertaining and surprisingly musical idea, which in its wit echoes the avant-garde tradition of Cage and György Ligeti (born 1923), is his *Clapping Music* (1972). The composer tells us that his idea was to create music with no instruments other than the human body, in this case the percussive nature of clapping. Reich divides the performers into two sections, one which sustains a constant rhythmic pattern in its clapping while the second section is directed to 'phase' its claps abruptly a beat ahead and at intervals continue advancing the beat until reaching a unison again within the first section.

With *Drumming* (1971) (for wordless voices, piccolo, four pairs of tuned bongo drums, three marimbas and three glockenspiels), Reich entered the field of large-scale composition in minimalist style—it lasts for one and a half hours—and succeeded in creating an apotheosis of percussive music making of symphonic proportions. The entire work is based on the repetition of a single rhythmic pattern. It is divided into four sections, though they are played without a break. Its scoring includes the voices of women who are used as if they were instruments; instead of words they are required to utter a mixture of consonant and vowel sounds.

During the 1970s and 1980s Reich consolidated his place not only among minimalist composers, but also on the contemporary musical scene in general with a series of compositions of ever increasing quality, both in terms of musical imagination and in maturity of craftsmanship. For example, apart from *Drumming*, from the 1970s, three works stand out—*Music for 18 Musicians* (1976), *Music for a Large Ensemble* (1978), the cheerful Octet—renamed as *Eight Lines for Chamber Orchestra* (1979). Of these, *Music for 18 Musicians* is perhaps the most striking with its strangely intoxicating combination of African, Balinese, Jazz and Western musical elements. Of the eighteen instrumentalists, four are female vocalists. Reich's adoption of the medieval organum and conductus (or long-note) techniques can on occasions give this music a majestic, archaic feel, although his use of the vibrato in the work does have the effect of evoking documentary nature-film music. But this observation serves as a reminder that in the universality of Reich's music-making, effects for film music are also a legitimate part of musico-semantics and it is up to us, the listeners, to decipher and absorb them.

The majestic tone which was already apparent in the *Music for 18 Musicians* was developed further by Reich during the first part of the 1980s, particularly in the *Variation for Wind, Strings and Keyboards* (1980). The conductus is also employed on a vast scale in this twenty-one or so minutes long elevating sound tableau, in which, among the other instruments, three electric organs emphatically underline the noble vision of the composer. And vision is indeed an operative word in Reich's musical world. His music possesses a visual attribute in the sense that light means something definite in musical terms for him; he sees light as "a metaphor for harmony, for tonality".[4]

There are two further outstanding works which have established the composer's reputation. The first of these is *Tehillim* (1981) of which there are two versions, chamber and orchestral. It is a setting of the nineteenth Psalm:

> The heavens declare the glory of God;
> And the firmament showeth his handiwork.
> Day unto day, uttereth speech,
> And night unto night showeth knowledge.
> There is no speech nor language,
> Where their voice is not heard . . .

The second work is the remarkable work for chorus and orchestra *Desert Music* (1983), a setting of sections of the American poet William Carlos Williams's collection of poems which appeared under the same title in 1954. It is a minimalist cantata in five movements, based on a symmetrical structuring of tempi: Fast–Moderate–Slow–Moderate–Slow–Moderate–Fast. Its cardinal lines are:

> Man has survived hitherto because he was too ignorant to know how to realize his wishes. Now that he can realize them, he must either change them or perish.[5]

It is likely to become a classic of contemporary American choral music.

Both his *Sextet* (1985) and *Six Marimbas* (1986) are brilliant handlings of percussive chamber ensembles, a type of chamber music-making which has by now established itself as a legitimate part of the contemporary performing repertoire. *Six Marimbas* is a re-scoring of an earlier work, *Six Pianos* (1973), but the *Sextet* is a relatively recent composition in which greater musical flexibility and variety is introduced and on occasions is even reminiscent of Bartók's Sonata for Two Pianos and Percussion (1937). Reich has established himself as a major figure in the minimalist camp.

Philip Glass (born 1937)

In his fascinating and informative book *Opera on the Beach*, Glass gives a vivid account not only of his own development as a composer, but also of the American and European artistic scene of the 1960s and 1970s. He writes of his involvement with 'progressive' theatre, of the New York downtown world of SoHo and of artists, musicians and performers.

Glass also received a most respectable academic education at the University of Chicago. This was followed by several years of further studies at the Juilliard School. Moreover, like so many American musicians before him, he too went to Paris where he became a devoted disciple of Nadia Boulanger from 1963 to 1965. It was in Paris that he encountered the great Indian sitar player, Ravi Shankar and was asked to transcribe Indian music to Western notation for Conrad Rook's psychedelic film-fantasy *Chappagna*.

Working with Ravi Shankar and also with the famous tabla player, Allah Rukha, over a sustained period opened a new world of music-making to Glass. The Indian raga system, but especially their use of rhythm was, as he declared, "a revelation" to him. What fascinated Glass was the entirely different way in which Indian musicians related to rhythm and time. He explains this simply and clearly:

> In Western music we divide time—as if you were to take a length of time and slice it the way you slice a loaf of bread. In Indian

music (and all the non-Western music with which I'm familiar),
you take small units, or "beats" and string them together to make
up larger time values.[6]

Before returning to America in 1965, Glass extended what he
had learnt from Ravi Shankar and Allah Rukha by travelling in
Africa, Central Asia and India. The importance of these experiences and the liberating influences of John Cage, pop music
with its amplified instruments and his involvement with the
avant-garde theatre can hardly be overstated. He was also
associated with an experimental group already established in
Paris, which became known as Mabou Mines. He acquired a
considerable familiarity with the theatre in general and with
Bertold Brecht and Samuel Beckett in particular, for whose *Play*
he wrote the incidental music in 1965. This was a composition
written for two soprano saxophones in truly minimalist style,
as the music is based on the repetition of the notes of only two
intervals but with rhythmic contrasts. The importance of theatre in the composer's musical thinking is best illustrated by
Glass's own statement:

> . . . from my earliest years as a composer there has always been a
> close bond between the music I have written for the theater and
> music for concert use. More often than not, theater was where my
> most innovative work began, often to be worked out and devel-
> oped later in my concert music.[7]

As we have seen already, some composers felt that the best
way to secure the performance of their music was to form their
own performing groups. Some, like Glass, even became
involved with the publication of their own works and by
founding recording companies and producing recordings.
Glass formed his own ensemble, under his own name, in 1968.
He gave performances with this ensemble in several galleries
and museums as well as in his own home on Sunday after-
noons. Referring to the early days of his composer-performing
career in a film interview, Glass recalls that " . . . to start with
there were only six people in the audience. One was my
mother and two others were friends".[8] This has gradually
changed and now, on occasion, the audience can number thou-
sands, not unlike a pop or rock concert.

Glass's musical style had established itself by the end of the 1960s. During that time he wrote works for the Glass Ensemble like *Music in Contrary Motion* (1969), *Music in Similar Motion* (1969)and *Music with Changing Parts* (1970). These compositions, together with one of his most popular pieces *Glassworks*, written much later in 1981 for the Glass Ensemble, show a progressive realisation of a style characterised by exuberant, hypnotic melodic and rhythmic repetitions in which Western musical tradition, rock and pop, are fused with elements of African and Indian music. The sheer elation which Glass is able to induce in his audience, for example in the 'Floe' section from *Glassworks*, is quite remarkable. It has an elemental, jubilatory force, not unlike the finale of Sibelius's Fifth Symphony with which it has some melodic affinity. Of the two existing versions, the one with solo soprano voice is arguably the more effective.

Minimalist music, largely because of its rhythmic richness and evocative nature, is singularly adaptable for dancing. Parts of *Glassworks*—'Rubric' and 'Facades'—were choreographed by Jerome Robbins together with the Funeral Music from his opera *Akhnaten* (1983) under the title *Glasspieces* in 1983.

Glass's music combines Young's mysticism with the essential minimalist cocktail of Indian, African, jazz/rock/pop and Western music. Added to this is some of the joy which is to be found in Reich's music and to which Glass contributes a somewhat sensuous vitality. Of such mixtures cults are made and to this state, Glass is rapidly progressing.

His long-standing involvement with avant-garde theatre and modern dance furnished him with an excellent grounding for the writing of opera—a form which he finds both intellectually and temperamentally congenial. Of the six operas written by Glass, the first three constitute a portrait trilogy based on the idea of writing a series of operas in which historical figures are the protagonists. Einstein was chosen for *Einstein on the Beach* (1975-1976) and Ghandi for *Satyagraha* (1980).

For *Akhnaten* (1983), Glass chose the lesser-known but fascinating resistance figure of the pharaoh Amenhotep IV who was martyred for his monotheistic religious reforms. In his preface to the libretto of *Akhnaten*, Glass compares this work with his other operas:

> *Einstein on the Beach*, an opera about a great mathematician who loved music, is for amplified ensemble and small chorus singing a text comprised of numbers (actually the beats of the music) and solfège syllables. *Satyagraha*, a work about one man leading his people to freedom, is a large choral opera with text taken directly from Gandhi's philosophical guidebook (the Bagavad-Gita) in the actual language (Sanskrit) in which he read it. In *Akhnaten*, my emphasis is orchestral, with choral and solo voices sharing common ground with the orchestra.[9]

The Ancient Egyptian setting of *Akhnaten* is singularly well-suited to the minimalist style, enabling the composer to give an impressive archaic grandeur to the whole composition. All three operas, and especially *Akhnaten*, possess a theatrical immediacy and lyrical warmth which distinguish Glass as a neo-romantic within the minimalist camp. It can, of course, be argued that the whole American minimalist school is fundamentally romantic. Within Glass's operatic triptych, connections are made by musical cross references, such as the bridging interludes called by the composer 'knee plays' in *Einstein on the Beach*, these reappearing as basic components in *Akhnaten* and helping to maintain both musical and theatrical unity.

This operatic triptych is an outstanding contribution to the modern operatic repertoire, or, more accurately, music theatre. In these works, Glass's craftsmanship, with his romantic temperament and an acute sense of drama are clearly seen. So too is his humanistic and social commitment, visible in the only way that an artist's socio-political stance is acceptable in a work of art without a degeneration into propaganda—by the integrity and intensity of a compassionate artistic vision projected by a universal humanity.

Glass has also ventured into writing film music. *Koyaanisqatsi* (1981) is notable for its powerful combination of images and music and for the absense of any spoken parts or story. The film offers a vision of contemporary life in which nature, technology and the idea of progress are seen in terms of a Hopi Indian prophecy, set to music, "If we dig precious things from the land, we will invite disaster".

Over the years, Glass has moulded his harmonic language towards greater flexibility and warmth producing moments of a strangely Bach-like harmonic timbre. This is a kind of neo-classicism which is much nearer to the Stravinsky of *Apollo Musagets* and *Le baiser de la fee* of the late 1920s than one would assume from the general style of Glass's work. Nowhere is this more strikingly so than *In the Upper Room* (1986), a score for the dance theatre of Twyla Tharp, and especially so in 1, 2 and 4. The third section ends abruptly—one of the many mannerisms of Glass's music which have such a striking effect. The ninth section is an ecstatic culmination in which the instrumental ensemble and synthesizers are joined by the voice of Dora Ohrenstein, who is now associated with the performing of Glass's music as Lotte Lenya was with Kurt Weill's.

As we have seen, Samuel Beckett's *Play* was amongst the first theatre works which left a deep impression on him and it was one for which he wrote incidental music. He has also composed incidental music in 1983 for Beckett's *Company* for the Mahon Mines experimental theatre group. This was scored for a four-movement string quartet. The title and tempo of each movement is indicated by a metronome mark alone (96, 160, 90 and 160 respectively). It is a melancholic work evoking the loneliness described in the text. In 1984 he also wrote the incidental music for Beckett's play *Endgame*.

In 1988 the American Repertory Company and Kentucky Opera commissioned and gave the first performance of his chamber opera, *The Fall of the House of Usher*. Debussy had intended to write an opera on Edgar Allan Poe's story but died before he could realise it. Glass's opera evokes the obsessive atmosphere of Poe's story of the death of a beautiful woman, a subject which the author believed to be "the most poetic topic in the world".

The reputation of Philip Glass as a contemporary master was further established when the Metropolitan Opera commissioned him to write an opera, *The Voyage*, premièred in

October 1992. He has come a long way since his time spent as a plumber and cab-driver to supplement his living and after many years of little recognition and much hostility. His career is a vindication of his integrity as a composer.

John Adams (born 1947)

The youngest of the minimalist quartet, John Adams, arrived onto the American and world musical scene with a mercurial élan as a fully-fledged composer during the late 1970s and early 1980s. Minimalism by that time was established as a major musical force and Adams was, of course, helped by the fact that the forerunners of the minimalist school had done much of the ground work. He had no sustained battle to fight for recognition as Reich and Glass had had before him. But Adams is only partially a minimalist and in fact he prefers not to be named among them as he sees himself as a romantic composer who uses certain characteristically minimalist features such as repetition of small units and strong sustained pulse.

A graduate and post-graduate in music at Harvard University, Adams gained his musical experience as a freelance clarinet player. He also studied conducting with Mario di Bonaventura and from 1972 to 1982 he was a teacher at the San Francisco Conservatory. During those years he became involved with the New Music Ensemble and initiated the New and Unusual Music Series. He gave up the prospect of an academic career to devote himself fully to composition. Since 1982 he has established himself as a leading American composer with a handful of outstanding compositions.

As a New Englander, like Charles Ives, Adams too was influenced by the Transcendentalists Ralph Waldo Emerson and Henry Thoreau who have contributed to the shaping of his romantic idealism and his attitude towards nature. His music, with its large scale poetic tableaux of space and time, has been influenced by the vast landscape of Northern California, a natural setting for the composer's contemplative nature.

It is noticeable that while most of the minimalists gained

their experience of melodic and rhythmic thinking via a close and sustained study of African, Indian and Balinese music, Adams absorbed the essentials of these influences directly from the works of the minimalists themselves. His departure point was where his minimalist forerunners had already arrived.

He found his voice as a composer in 1977 with the piano composition *China Gates* (1977). This repetitive piece of music goes through several keys, not via the customary modulations, but through what the composer calls 'gates'. The sustaining pedal is held throughout each section up to the 'gating', where the new key starts, and so on until the end. The constantly and methodically changing patterns of the same notes in each bar give the music a shimmering, hypnotic effect.

Phrygian Gates (1977–1978), also for solo piano, is in principle similar to *China Gates*, but conceived on a much more ambitious scale. The score consists of some sixty pages of relentlessly pulsating rhythms, as well as a series of massive chords, especially between bars 640–808. At the end, the music is left to ring in the air and gradually fade away, as in some Oriental music, or as in the case of Béla Bartók's Sonata for Two Pianos and Percussion (1937). Already, in these early pieces, it is evident that Adams's interest in minimalism rests on pulsation, subtle rhythmic and melodic patterns leading to larger units and on tonality. To a lesser extent his interest also includes modality-orientated harmonic and melodic styles. As opposed to some of his fellow minimalists, however, his music is conceived in a 'thorough-composed' manner and is meticulously written out on conventionally notated scores.

The string septet *Shaker Loops* (1978) is a spirited evocation of the behaviour of members of the Millennial Church, which originated in eighteenth-century England and now only worships in America. They practised celibacy and the sharing of property but above all, they were known by their ecstatic shaking during worship. Adams's playfulness reveals itself in the use of the minimalist style to refer to the shaking, as well as emphasising the effect by looping the tapes, a technique learnt during his early interest in electronic music. There are four movements: 'Shaking and Trembling', 'Hymning Slews', 'Loops and Verses' and 'Final Shaking'. It would be a mistake to hear in this music only wit, a musical *jeu d'esprit*, as it reveals not only brilliant compositional skill, but a romantic lyricism, which remains one of the endearing characteristics of Adams's music. A version for a string orchestra appeared in 1983.

With the *Common Tones in Simple Time* (1979) he turned to orchestral writing and with *Harmonium* (1981), to the combination of a large orchestra and a vast chorus. *Harmonium* is a setting of 'Negative Love', one of the strangest poems of John Donne, and two passionate poems by the great American poet Emily Dickinson: 'Because I could not stop for Death' and 'Wild nights—wild nights!'. In this work Adams pulled out all the stops—its lyrical content is combined with a majestic spaciousness and an unashamed romantic immediacy.

For some time now among musicologists, it has been a taboo to refer to feelings in connection with one of the most emotion-orientated forms of art, music. Yet, the minimalists, above all Philip Glass and John Adams, trigger off in us an immediate elemental response which has had no parallel for decades in the modern, so called 'serious' musical scene. This is a factor which must be taken into account when discussing their music. The trigger in the concert hall responses is as direct as those often engendered by jazz, or by rock and pop music. But, whereas in pop, for example, the level of intoxication seldom goes beyond the youth-orientated socio-sexual level, minimalist music, on the other hand, enters the realm of spiritual elevation via an already familiar route: tonality-based romanticism. It has been stated that "Romanticism is perhaps more in the mind of the listener than in the mind of the composer . . ."[10] Adams contradicts this statement, by preferring to be seen primarily as a romantic composer rather than as a minimalist and indeed his roots, more than any other of the minimalists, are in the romantic tradition.

Grand Pianola Music (1982) was Adams's venture into a highly individual kind of concerto style. It is scored for two pianos, wind and percussion instruments, as well as for soprano voices, singing wordless music in the earlier movements. Interesting effects are created by his use of the bass drum, with its crashing impact and especially by simulating the pianola sound by making the two pianists play the same music, but just out of phase.

A much more impressive orchestral work, with an intellectual and emotional intensity comparable to *Harmonium*, is *Harmonielehre* (1984–1985). In this composition, Adams's singular ability to create a sense of spaciousness, a vast shimmering musical landscape, as it were, of distance, light and time, is revealed.

More recently, he has achieved notoriety with a truly contemporary opera *Nixon in China* (1987). Based on a libretto of the poet Alice Goodman, the opera takes for its subject the historic visit to China by President Nixon in 1972 and his meeting with Chairman Mao. Together with the librettist and the producer Peter Sellars, Adams succeeded superbly in making a contemporary political opera in which the banal grandeur and empty exchanges of political encounters, such as Nixon's arrival at the airport or the banquet scene in Act 1, achieve a great dramatic power. Nixon's arrival aria is turned minimalist by sheer repetition: "News news news news news news news news news news news news has a has a has a has a kind of mystery has a has a has a kind of mystery . . ." This is both funny and critical in its reflection of the hollow megalomaniacal euphoria of the occasion. Perhaps the least convincing moment is in the third act where an idealised Chou En-Lai waxes poetic, but the music is outstanding throughout. The headiness of the banquet scene with its heavy brass section, or the crude second scene of Act Two, where the guests are watching the ballet, The Red Detachment of Women, written by Chiang Chiang, wife of Chairman Mao, and in which Henry Kissinger suddenly appears as a cruel landlord, are memorable theatrical moments, both dramatically and musically. But this remarkable opera should not be seen as a caricature of the rapprochement between America and China. The librettist and composer made this opera work on the level of human tragedy.

The Death of Klinghoffer, Adams's second opera, was completed in 1991 and given its première at the Théatre Royal de la

Monnaie in Brussels. Collaborating again with the librettist Alice Goodman and the director Peter Sellars, Adams based his subject, like *Nixon in China*, on contemporary political events. The story is centred on the murder by terrorists of Leon Klinghoffer, a passenger, confined to a wheelchair, on board the hijacked Italian cruise liner Achille Lauro in 1985. This brutal event is elaborated by the librettist and Adams into a twentieth-century passio-opera in which the suffering of both Palestinians and Jews together with the martyrdom of Klinghoffer become a lament on the human capacity for inflicting infinite suffering. Indeed, Adams stated that the model for this opera was not to be found in other operas but rather in Bach's Passion settings.

The opera begins with a Prologue, divided into two parts. This first part is given to the Chorus of Exiled Palestinians:

> My father's house was razed
> In nineteen forty-eight
> When the Israelis passed
> Over our street . . .

The second part is given to the Chorus of the Exiled Jews:

> When I paid of the taxi I had no money left and, of course, no luggage. My empty hands shall signify this passion, which itself remembers.

The tragedy then unfolds in two acts, consisting of five scenes in all. Not unlike Bach's Passions or classical Greek dramas, the choruses, given headings such as 'Ocean chorus', 'Night chorus' and 'Desert chorus', serve as commentators as well as protagonists .

The work ends with the captain of the ship telling the wife of Leon Klinghoffer that her husband was thrown overboard in the wheelchair. Her heartrending solo of rage and lament ends with the following words:

> If a hundred
> people were murdered
> And their blood
> Flowed in the wake
> Of this ship like
> Oil, only then
> Would the world intervene.

> They should have killed me.
> I wanted to die.

The poetic lyricism and the dramatic intensity of these and other sections of the opera firmly establish Adam's standing not only as one of the foremost composers of our time, but also as one who is a compassionate witness of the shames of our time.

The oratorio-like style of this strange opera makes it singularly successful as a recording. It has an immediacy and comprehensibility which can be absorbed without necessarily seeing it on the stage. This may seem a strange thing to say about an opera which was, after all, meant to be visually absorbed. Adams, yet again, has succeeded in suprising us with his moving amalgamation of passion-oratorio and opera. There can be little doubt that Adams is a major figure on the contemporary musical scene whose next composition is awaited with interest.

Minimalism, an almost naïve return to tonality and to the romantically sensuous, is now a powerful force in music and will certainly have a lasting influence. After the apparent dead-end of serialism, there is a popular euphoria for minimalism. Its language, which was criticised to begin with as being limited, turns out to be more flexible and much richer than its first critics thought possible. It has become a truly American music, but, at the same time, it is also an idiom that easily crosses borders. From its beginnings in the milieu of alternative culture, it has entered the prestigious concert halls and opera houses of the world.

Three Latin American Masters:
Heitor Villa-Lobos, Carlos Chavez
and Mauricio Kagel

Please, have fresh ears!
Mauricio Kagel

NO BOOK WRITTEN ON AMERICAN MUSIC CAN ignore the musical contribution made by the growing number of outstanding Latin American composers, whose musical activities have reached well beyond the frontiers of their countries. This is indeed an achievement considering the overwhelming economic, social and political turmoil handicapping Latin America to this day. It is worthy of note, however, that the idea and practice of the state's duty to finance and encourage the arts is wide-spread in Latin American countries. From the many names representing a possible cross-section of Latin American music—short of giving a country by country account which would be beyond the scope of this book—there are three composers who have been chosen by reason of their international repute. Of these, the most renowned is arguably Villa-Lobos and the most notorious, Mauricio Kagel.

Heitor Villa-Lobos (1887–1959)

In general terms, Latin American musical culture can be characterised as an amalgamation of three distinct influences: native Indian, European (i.e. Spanish, Portuguese and French) and, through the slave trade, African. The country in which these elements are perhaps best blended is Brazil, the native country of Villa-Lobos, who was born in Rio de Janeiro. His basic musical education was founded on the teaching of his father, who was an amateur musician. He learned to play the cello and piano but composition came naturally, as it were, without any formal instruction. Indeed, any academic discipline seems to have been contrary to his temperament, so consequently, what he learned was self-taught. Travelling and collecting folk and popular music, especially Indian music, of his native country was a rich and rewarding experience for him. What he found, melodically and rhythmically, he absorbed into his music and made his own. So much so, that in Villa-Lobos's music, an indigenous Brazilian musical style is evoked both in spirit and often in practice—he incorporated Indian folk instruments into his orchestration, for example in the three dances of *Dansas Africanas: Dances of Mestico Indians of Brazil* (1914).

For a considerable time he was able to stay in Paris on a government grant, but characteristically, as a composer he learned little from the cultural upsurge of Europe in the 1920s. He remained the same stubbornly individualistic Villa-Lobos. He even went as far as to say that he had not come to Paris in order to learn about French music, but to introduce them to his own.

He took up conducting which he practised extensively both in Brazil and the United States. But his most remarkable venture was when he turned his attention to the musical education of his own country. As a director of musical education, first in Saõ Paulo (1930–1932) and then from 1932 in Rio de Janeiro, he undertook the mammoth task of reorganising musical education. He introduced the learning and singing of Brazilian folksongs in schools and initiated a nationwide choral singing movement. He also invented a method of hand-signals which enabled the musically illiterate to read music relatively quickly. His impact on Brazilian musical education was quite phenomenal and comparable to Zoltán Kodály's in Hungary.

As a composer he was incredibly prolific. He wrote over two thousand works including twelve symphonies, seventeen string quartets and three operas. Of those which are available in Europe, not all are of an equal standard as he tended to write quickly and with an unashamed sentimentality, a kind of

Brazilian schmaltz. But some of his best compositions, which appeared over many years under two collective names: *Choros* and *Bachianas brasileiras*, possess a lasting musical vision. In them he succeeded in demonstrating the very essence of the music of his beloved country, of which he had such a singular understanding. *Choros* is a term denoting street band musicians who played dance tunes. Inspired by their existence, he composed several instrumental works for differing forces, from chamber to orchestral music, during the 1920s. *Bachianas brasileiras* contains a series of compositions in which a strange attempt was made by the composer to amalgamate the Baroque contrapuntal style, exemplified by J. S. Bach, with Brazilian folk music. This was based on his strong belief that Bach's musical thinking and indigenous Brazilian music had some affinity. He kept working at intervals in this style between 1930–1945. One of the most popular in this series, if not of all his compositions, is no. 5 for soprano and eight cellos (1938–1945).

Villa-Lobos primarily saw himself as a nationalist composer, who had duties to his nation which he served with indefatigable energy all his life. As he stated:

> I am a nationalist, but not a patrioteer. The distinction is most important. Patriotism in music and capitalizing upon it, is very dangerous. You cannot produce great music in that way. You will have instead propaganda. But nationalism—power of the earth, the geographic and ethnographic influences that a composer cannot escape; the musical idioms and sentiment of people and environment—these origins, in my opinion, are indispensable to a vital and genuine art.[1]

Carlos Chavez (1899–1978)

For the Mexicans, Carlos Chavez is for music what the better known nationalist-revolutionary painter Diego Rivera is for art. Chavez was brought up in the very midst of the Mexican Revolution—the uprising against Porfirio Diaz, led by Francesco Madera in 1911, eventually leading to the creation of a democratic constitution in 1917 which is still to be realised.

These were times of considerable upheaval and change which left a deep impression on his outlook. Like Villa-Lobos, he too turned to the native soil, ". . . to the musical idioms and sentiment of the people and environment . . ." by assimilating his own country's indigenous musical heritage. Chavez's music is harsher, more robust in tone than that of Villa-Lobos. This may be because of his greater involvement with contemporary compositional developments. During his visit to Europe in 1922–1923, he encountered modernism in full swing. This affected his musical thinking much more than Villa-Lobos, who, as we have seen, remained relatively indifferent. Returning to Mexico he initiated concert series under the title Música Nueva, giving performances of works by Eric Satie, Igor Stravinsky and other modernists for the first time in Mexico. Chavez's musical style could be summarised as being neo-primitive, corresponding to Stravinsky's *Rite of Spring* period. To achieve this, he put emphasis not only on Mexican instruments in general but on percussive instruments in particular, such as in *Toccata for Percussion Instruments* (1942). Like Villa-Lobos, he also turned to conducting and teaching, including the administration of educational policies both in his capacities as conductor of the Orchestra Sinfónica de Mexico and as the director of the National Conservatory of Music. In these capacities, he played a major role in the cultural and educational evolution of Mexico.

From the time of his writing the ballet *E fuego nuevo* (1921) to his *Sinfonia Indiano* (1939), Chavez pursued the style of neo-primitive nationalism. But from the late 1930s onwards he adopted, largely for ideological reasons, the neo-classical style. In order to make his music more accessible, he started to write in a less pronounced modernistic vein than that of his first period. One ideal which had a permanent place in his ars poetica was the desire to use his art as a mirror for the life of Mexican people. This resulted in a Mexican version of socialist realist art, an idea which was also close to his friend and artistic collaborator Diego Rivera. His second ballet *H. P.* (horse power) (1932) was intended by both the composer and Rivera, who collaborated in the production of the ballet, as a criticism of the modern machine age against which the workers in the ballet rebel. The capitalist exploiters are ousted and human equilibrium is regained by the workers taking control of the machines for the benefit of all. In this context it should also be remembered that Chavez, who initiated concerts for the propagation of modern music, was also the founder of Conciertos para Trabajadores—Concerts for Workers in 1930. To this genre belongs the *Sinfonia Proletariat* (1934) with its references to proletarian revolution. The piano score of *Sinfonia Proletariat* was lavishly illustrated by Rivera.

Chavez's musical language, in spite of striving to be direct and immediately comprehensible for ideological reasons, is on the whole sophisticated and modern and not as immediate as some of his fanciful programmatic titles would indicate. He was after all a modernist in whose music sentimentality and overt emotion have little place. Henry Cowell, the North American modernist, was of the opinion that Chavez wrote the only music worth listening to in Latin America—an exaggerated view, but considering its source, one which throws some light on Chavez's standing.

One of the most impressive works of his late period is his Sixth Symphony (1963), which received its première under Leonard Bernstein. From this period also comes the work *Soli*, the culmination of thirty years of involvement with a series of works for wind instruments. In these compositions each instrument plays a solo role in one of the movements, thus combining ensemble music with the idea of solo playing. The inherent concerto principle in this method led him to extend the idea to a 'soli' for orchestra and four soloists in *Soli III* (1965).

The neglect of marginalised nations, exacerbated by a patronising ignorance is, on occasion, followed by a sudden discovery and over-enthusiastic appraisal by the rest of the Western world. Thus Chavez, representing the very spirit of Mexico, found himself inundated with honours, from the Legion of Honour to the distinction of Commander, Order of the Polar Star from Sweden. A more modest, but penetrating assessment of his status was written by a fellow composer

Aaron Copland, who, in his brilliant short book on modern music, wrote:

> . . . His music embodies almost all the major traits of modern music: the rejection of Germanic ideals, the objectification of senti-ment, the use of folk material in its relation to nationalism, the intricate rhythms, linear as opposed to vertical writing, the specif-ically 'modern' sound images. It is music that belongs entirely to our own age. It propounds no problems, no metaphysics. Chavez' music is extraordinarily healthy. It is music created not as a sub-stitute for living but as a manifestation of life. It is clear and clean-sounding, without shadows or softness. Here is contemporary music if ever there was any.[2]

Mauricio Kagel (born 1931)

Mauricio Kagel was born in Argentina, Buenos Aires, where he studied several instruments as well as singing and conducting. But as a composer he was self-taught. His wide-ranging inter-ests led him to literature, philosophy, theatre and film. These diverse genres impressed upon him not so much the differ-ences between the arts, but rather their interaction. For him, music is only a part of the totality of available expressions, although having a cardinal role, one well beyond its traditional confines. Consequently, in his highly idiosyncratic world of artistic happenings, Kagel's approach to theatre or film is musical, while his approach to music may be, when he wishes, theatrical and visual.

Kagel resists being labelled yet his art inescapably reminds us of aspects of expressionism, dadaism and surrealism. He belongs belatedly to the surrealist fraternity of André Breton, Salvador Dalí and Luis Buñuel. It is not by accident that in 1982 he wrote music for a reissue of the surrealist silent film of 1928, *Un Chien andalou* by Buñuel and Dalí—an undertaking which Kagel carried out with impeccable stylistic devotion and insight.

The many musical influences which have shaped Kagels's thinking include aspects of the serial techniques of the Second Viennese School and of the music of Kurt Weill of the

Brecht/Weill period, Eric Satie as well as John Cage, and the Cologne avant-garde of the 1960s and 1970s headed by Karlheinz Stockhausen. Lately, some signs of a new influence, the minimalist style, have also crept into Kagel's musical vocabulary, an influence that can be detected in his *An Tasten* (1988), an effective romantic étude for piano.

His compositions, whether written for purely instrumental music, music-theatre or films, are characterised by originality of imagination, wit and a twisted sense of ironic humour, but behind which lurks a jovial, romantic temperament. In his works everything can contribute to music-making from sighing, as in *Siegfried/P* (1988), to the tapping of walking-sticks in *Pas de Cinq* (1965), to the rhythmically banged chair in *Dressur* (1986). The techniques of chance and collage are also part of this indefatigable and resourceful teaser's compositional style, as in the case of *Heterophonie* (1959–1961), where independent music is distributed around several ensembles formed out of forty-two musicians, all to be performed jointly.

His interest in film, silent and surrealist films in general and those made by Buñuel in particular, combined with his ideas of the interrelationship of the arts, has led him towards film-making. In Kagel's films, music plays such an important role that they might as well be seen and heard as musical compositions. As both art forms rely heavily on time sequence—one, which is visually perceived and has the added advantage of being able to deal with concrete ideas, the other, abstract and being able to communicate via feelings—Kagel offers a synthesis of music, theatre and film. *Antithese* (1965) opened a series of films, now numbering almost twenty, in which his synthetic approach was realised. The music is based on electronic sound effects which blend in with the manic behaviour of a technician, who goes berserk in a studio packed with abandoned machines of all kinds, such as record players, radios and tape-recorders. *Match* (1966) is a surrealist chamber piece combining film and music in which two cellists and an umpire playing percussion instruments are having a contest. The humour of this work, in common with many of these creations of Kagel's, possess a disarming charm.

Hallelujah (1967–1969) is perhaps one of his densest compositions and the one most indebted to Buñuel's *Un Chien andalou* in its surrealist technique and imagery. A real surrealist fantasy, it has multiple layers, combining the humorous with the near nightmarish. A particularly clever idea is his use of an anatomy lesson in which medical statements concerning the functioning of the larynx modulate into voice practising which includes the uttering of the word 'Hallelujah'.

Kagel's talent for stylish mocking inevitably found a musical target. The victim was Beethoven in *Ludwig van* (1969–1970) where, using the Beethoven's music, Kagel's surrealism shows the distortions that time has made between Beethoven's own period and ours.

At this point, it is perhaps appropriate to mention that in 1957 Kagel decided to leave Argentina in order to settle in Cologne, Germany for good. In a relatively recent interview, he expressed his view that as a musician he is an international being and that nationality has far less importance, as far as he is concerned at any rate, than it is generally assumed.

His continuing interest in silent films resulted in the composition *M. M. 51* (1981). The title is the indication of a metronome setting. While the metronome ticks relentlessly at 51 beats per minute, a pianist plays Kagel's expressionist horror-film music. The pianist must also laugh menacingly to add to the terror. The piece ends with the pianist's muted shout frozen on his open-mouthed face, reminiscent of Edvard Munch's famous etching 'The Shout'. The very same piece was used by the composer as an accompaniment to F. W. Murnau's classic silent film *Nosferatu, eine Symphonie des Grauens* (*Nosferatu, a Symphony of Terror*) (1922). Kagel's film version under the title *M. M. 51/Nosferatu* (1981–1983) is a stylish *jeu d'ésprit*.

Dressur (1986), an instrumental film/theatre piece, is set in a circus ring, an image liked and used by many artists, such as Toulouse Lautrec, Auguste Renoir, Pablo Picasso, Eric Satie, Federico Fellini and many others, for its colourful symbolic significance. The three musicians in *Dressur* are called upon to play on percussion instruments from the conventional xylophone to Dutch clogs, continental carpet-beater and half coconut shells (which are rhythmically knocked against the bare belly of one of the performers). The three percussionists are also clowns, as they move around with rhythmic deliberation within the confinement of their circus ring. As so often with the circus, at the end of a show one is left with the simultaneous emotional state of bewildered cheerfulness and profound sadness. Kagel's *Dressur* conjures up this ambivalent feeling from one's childhood.

The above examples, selected from a much larger body of works, give an impression of the nature of Kagel's art, in which the absurd and banal, the visual and aural are brought together with great sophistication, often within the framework of music-theatre and film compositions. He is an Argentinian surrealist, *enfant terrible* in the disguise of a German burger, a man of the theatre and film dominated by music, or vice versa, an uprooted jester, who, like Beckett—a favourite writer of his—arouses in us a strange world of existential happenings. Kagel relies as much on the stage as Beckett does on music. They meet at the point where the only right articulation is sound followed by silence while a mute metronome is ticking on and on.

Epilogue

I hear America singing, the varied carols I hear.
Walt Whitman

T HE CREATIVITY OF THE MUSICAL LIFE OF BOTH North and Latin America is continually changing and developing, and it does so within the framework of interacting multi-cultural traditions.

How much American musical life has also been shaped and enriched by the influx of refugee musicians from the 1930s onwards cannot be quantified. There can be little doubt however that American musicology, for example, was founded on works of the largely Austro-German émigré musicologists who settled there for good. Such names as Gustave Reese, Paul Henry Lang, Alfred Einstein and Curt Sachs come immediately to mind. In terms of composition the problem is much more complex but it is certain, however, that the impact of America on those who emigrated there, was considerable both in the positive and negative sense. Béla Bartók, for instance, wrote some of his most important scores—such as Concerto for Orchestra (1943), *Sonata for unaccompanied violin* (1944) and the Piano Concerto no. 3 (1945)—while in exile from 1940 to his death in 1945. They are profound expressions of his musical vision, combining a moral and artistic integrity deeply rooted in Middle and Western European traditions. Kurt Weill, on the other hand, abandoned his bitter-sweet, socially committed concert-cabaret style of the Weimar Republic for the sentimental style of Broadway musicals. This of course may have been the direct result of economic pressures precipitated by the Second World War. It was also arguably a loss for music. It should never be forgotten that the émigrés and refugees who left a Europe, where they had been persecuted for their political beliefs and race, did so in the hope of being able to carry on living and working in relative freedom. This they were able to do in spite of the many difficulties and hardships they faced.

The so-called 'hard times' of Béla Bartók in America are incomparable to the nightmare which the Fascists and later the Stalinists provided for millions of innocent citizens who could not or did not want to get away from war-torn Europe. Yet, it is not easy to be an exile for this too has its own terror. Some made the adjustment and were able to assimilate for better or worse, like Kurt Weill and Erns Krenek. Others, as was the case with Bartók, weathered it with nostalgic longing in the hope of returning one day to their mother-country. A few were not too perturbed, like Igor Stravinsky, as they were already accustomed to a cosmopolitan lifestyle. The presence of such eminent musical personalities—the list is an impressive one, including composers such as Arnold Schoenberg and Paul Hindemith—has left its mark on American musical life, as we have already seen in the case of John Cage or George Crumb, to mention only two.

The fact that so many chose to emigrate to America in this century has a symbolic significance in the sense that, during a tragic period of European and world history, America represented a haven for those who were oppressed. This fact cannot be diminished even by such tragic episodes as the shameful McCarthy era, and the many unresolved socio-economical and racial problems affecting American life to this day.

Musically, America has grown into maturity and, in the hands of a succession of composers, has succeeded in forging a language which is unmistakably its own. This has been achieved within a relatively short time-span and largely by absorbing different ways of music-making from all over the globe. The music of composers such as Charles Ives, George Gershwin, John Cage, Philip Glass and John Adams, offers us statements in sound which could only have been made by Americans. Minimalism, to give a relatively recent example became one of the most promising musical developments since the post-Webern serialism school and the electronic music makers. There can be little doubt that some of the works, for instance, John Adams's *Harmonium* and *Nixon in China*, are already classics of our time. It is always a dangerous thing and perhaps even futile to look into a crystal-ball in order to predict what is likely to happen in the future, whether in the arts or elsewhere. Yet, one may venture to suggest that a likely development is the further growth of an international style characterised by an increasing absorption of both Western and Oriental music, mixing with these jazz, pop/rock and 'serious' styles. In other words, a synthetic approach to music is likely to be a dominant development both in America and beyond. A re-evaluation of the romantic style in late twentieth-century terms is already in full swing. Neo-romanticism is clearly apparent in the works of such composers as John Adams in America, Peter Maxwell Davies in Britain, and György Ligeti in Continental Europe. With the disintegration of monolithic states, a return to nationalistic interests are likely to bring a mushrooming of identity-conscious music based on folk materials. Further exploration in the field of electronic music continues to offer a vast mine of potential. So too the works of women composers are increasingly likely to be heard as the male domination of the musical world rapidly changes. (It is notable, however, that in a recent book on American composers in conversation, out of twenty-five composers interviewed only four were women, and one of these, Laurie Anderson, is in fact regarded as being a performance artist and pop musician.) There can be no doubt that American musicians will be in the forefront of a musical creativity characterised by an uninhibited flair for experimentation.

American music, whether in the fields of jazz, popular music or concert music, has progressed to the forefront of contemporary musical culture—no mean achievement since the time of Alexis de Tocqueville's devastating observation, quoted at the beginning of this book, concerning the state of America's culture in the early 1830s.

Notes

Chapter 1: Background, Part 1

1. Alexis de Tocqueville, *Democracy in America* (New York: Random House, 1948), p. 326. See also Alexis de Tocqueville, *Democracy in America* (New York: Harper and Row, 1966), pp. 277–278.
2. A term aptly used by Professor H. W. Hitchcock in *Music in the United States: A Historical Introduction* (New Jersey: Prentice-Hall, 1969), p. 51.

Chapter 2: Businessman and Musical Genius: Charles Ives

1. *Twentieth Century Composers 1, American Music Since 1910* (London: Weidenfeld & Nicolson, 1970), p. 30.
2. Wilfred Mellers, *Music in a New Found Land: Themes and Developments in the History of American Music* (London: Barrie and Rockliff, 1964), p. 56.
3. R. S. Perry, *Charles Ives and the American Mind* (Ohio: Kent State University Press, 1974), p. 65.

Chapter 3: Background, Part 2

1. The term 'popular' in music dictionaries excludes 'serious' or classical music, folk music and jazz. There are also types of religious music, such as the spiritual and the Gospel song which, while not generally categorised as popular music, because of their folk roots and popularity could rightfully be included under this term. The traditional polarising titles 'serious' music and 'light' music are out of fashion nowadays because of the blurring of their distinctions, especially in modern music. The matter is further complicated by the use of the term 'popular' when a 'serious' or classical composition happens to be so, even though it is excluded from the genre of popular music. In this book, the term is not used in its narrow or exclusive sense, but in a more general way including spiritual music, Gospel songs and jazz.
2. The 'cake walk' was a plantation dance performed by black slaves which became popular around the 1890s.

Chapter 6: Baked by Nadia Boulanger: Aaron Copland

1. Alex Harman and Wilfrid Mellers, *Man and His Music* (London: Barrie and Rockliff, 1962), p. 1058.

Chapter 7: A Frenchman in New York: Edgard Varèse

1. Louise Varèse, *A Looking-Glass Diary*, vol. 1: 1883–1928 (London: Eulenburg Books, 1975), p. 121.

2. ibid.
3. ibid.
4. ibid, p. 122.
5. *Christian Science Monitor*, 8 July 1922.
6. Igor Stravinsky, "Some Composers", *Musical America*, June 1962, p. 11.
7. Jean Petit, *Poeme Electronique Le Corbusier* (Paris: Editions de Minuit, 1959), p. 192.
8. 'Varèse envisions "Space" Symphonies', *New York Times*, 6 December 1936.
9. Odile Vivier, 'Les Innovations Instrumentales d'Edgard Varèse', *La Revue Musical* (Paris), no. 226 (1955). Quoted (trans. by Derek Coltman) in Fernard Quellette, *Edgard Varèse* (London: Calder & Boyers, 1968), p. 91.
10. Edgard Varèse quoted in Elliott Schwartz and Barney Childs, eds., *Contemporary Composers on Contemporary Music* (New York: Holt, Reinhart & Winston, 1967), p. 203.
11. Composer's notes to recording, 1954.
12. Honoré de Balzac, *Gambara* (Paris: Garmien-Flammarion, 1981), p. 137 (author's translation).

Chapter 8: Gambling with Sounds and Silence: John Cage

1. Umbro Apollonio, ed., *Futurist Manifestos* (London: Thames and Hudson, 1973), p. 75.
2. Charles Hamm, 'Sound Forms for Piano', notes for *Recorded Anthology of American Music*, no. 203, New World Records, p. 5.

Chapter 9: Some Modernist Front-Runners

1. Roger Sessions, edited by Edward T. Cone, *Roger Sessions on Music: Collected Essays* (Princeton: Princeton University Press, 1979) p. 165.
2. ibid., p. 164.
3. Mellers (1964), p. 135.
4. ibid., p. 301.
5. ibid., p. 294.
6. Harry Parch, *Genesis of Music*, revised and enlarged edition (New York: Da Capo Press, 1974), p. 9.
7. ibid., p. 32.
8. Charles Hamm, *Music in the New World* (New York: Norton, 1983), p. 597.
9. Susanne K. Langer, *Feeling and Form: A Theory of Art* (London: Routledge & Kegan Paul, 1953), p. 109.
10. Else Stone and Kurt Stone, ed., *The Writings of Elliott Carter* (Indiana: Indiana University Press, 1977), p. 272.
11. ibid., p. 276–7.

12. ibid., p. 277.

13. ibid., p. 273.

14. ibid., p. 275.

15. ibid.

16. Milton Babbitt, 'Twelve-tone rhythmic structure and the electronic medium', in *Perspective of New Music* (Princeton: Princeton University Press, 1962), p. 49.

17. Earle Brown, *Hodograph 1*. Composer's notes to recording, 1959.

18. Richard Steinitz, 'The Music of George Crumb', *Contact*, no. 11 (1975): p. 16.

Chapter 10: The American Minimalists

1. A movement uniting a diverse range of artists, including musicians, wishing to express themselves in alternative experimental forms.

2. Paul Griffiths, *Modern Music, The Avant-Garde Since 1945* (London: Dent, 1981), p. 176

3. Steve Reich, *Early Works* (Electra/Asylum/Nonesuch Records, 1987).

4. Steve Reich in conversation with Jonathon Cott (Electra/Asylum/Nonesuch Records, New York, 1985).

5. Steve Reich, *Desert Music*, 1983.

6. Philip Glass, *Opera on the Beach: Philip Glass on his new world of music theatre* (London: Faber & Faber, 1988), p. 17.

7. ibid., p. 19.

8. *Philip Glass*, a film by Peter Greenaway (Transatlantic Films, 1985).

9. Philip Glass, *Akhnaten* (CBS Records 'Masterworks', 01–042457 –20/M3 42457, 1987).

10. Paul Griffiths, *The Thames and Hudson Encyclopedia of 20th-Century Music* (London: Thames & Hudson, 1986) p. 128.

Chapter 11: Three Latin American Masters

1. Heitor Villa-Lobos, interviews in *The Christian Science Monitor* and *The New York Times*, quoted in David Ewen, ed., *The New Book of Modern Composers: 'The Composer Speaks'*, (New York: Alfred A Knopf, 1972), p. 437.

2. Aaron Copland, *The New Music 1900–1960* (New York: W. W. Norton & Co., 1968), p. 145–146.

Select Bibliography

Battcock, Gregory, ed. *Breaking the Sound Barrier: A Critical Anthology of the New Music.* New York: E. P. Dutton, 1981.

Brindle, Reginald Smith. *The New Music: The Avant-Garde Since 1945.* Oxford: Oxford University Press, 1975.

Chase, Gilbert. *America's Music.* New York: McGraw-Hill Book Company, 1966.

Chase, Gilbert, ed. *The American Composers Speak: A Historical Anthology 1770–1965.* Louisiana: Louisiana State University Press, 1966.

Citron, Marcia. *Gender and the Music Canon.* Cambridge: Cambridge University Press, 1993.

Cook, Susan C., and Judy S. Tsou. *Cecilia Reclaimed: Feminist Perspective on Gender and Music.* Urbana and Chicago: University of Illinois Press, 1994.

Cowell, Henry, ed. *American Composers on American Music.* Standford: Standford University Press, 1933.

Ewen, David. *Composers Since 1900. A Biographical and Critical Guide.* New York: The H. W. Wilson Company, 1969.

Fuller, Sophie. *The Pandora Guide to Women Composers: Britain and the United States 1629 – Present.* London: Pandora, 1994.

Gayne, Cole, and Trace Caras. *Soundpieces: Interviews with American Composers.* Metuchen, New Jersey: Scarecrow Press, 1982.

Glass, Philip. *Opera on the Beach.* London: Faber & Faber, 1988.

Griffiths, Paul. *A Guide to Electronic Music.* London: Thames & Hudson, 1979.

———. *Modern Music: The Avant-Garde Since 1945.* London: Dent & Sons Ltd, 1981.

———. *The Thames and Hudson Encyclopedia of 20th Century Music.* London: Thames & Hudson, 1986.

Hamm, Charles. *Music in the New World.* New York :W. W. Norton & Company, 1983.

Hitchcock, H.,Wiley. *Music in the United States: A Historical Introduction.* New Jersey: Prentice-Hall, 1969, 1974.

Hitchcock, H., Wiley and Stanley Sadie, eds. *The New Grove Dictionary of American Music.* London: Macmillan Publishing Ltd., 1986.

Lowens, Irving. *Music and Musicians in Early America.* New York: W. W. Norton and Company, 1964.

Mellers, Wilfred. *Music in a New Found Land: Themes and Developments in the History of American Music.* London: Barrie & Rockliff, 1964

Rockwell, John. *All American Music: Composition in the Late Twentieth Century.* London: Kahn & Averill, 1983.

Sadie, Julie Anne and Rhian Samuel, eds. *The New Grove Dictionary of Women Composers.* London: Macmillan Publishing Ltd. 1994

Sadie, Stanley, ed. *The New Grove Dictionary of Music.* London: Macmillan Publishing Ltd., 1980.

Slonimsky, Nicolas. *Music of Latin America.* New York: Da Capo Press, 1972.

Smith, Geoff, and Nicola Walker Smith. *American Originals.* London: Faber & Faber, 1994.

Thomson, Virgil. *Twentieth Century Composers: I. American Music Since 1900.* London: Weidenfeld and Nicolson, 1970.

Discography

The following guides and mail order companies may help readers locate recordings of the works discussed in this book.

Cook, Richard and Brian Morlan. *The Penguin Guide to Jazz.* Harmondsworth: Penguin Books, 1995.

Glassen, Stanley. *Classic FM A-Z of Classical Music.* London: Headline Book Publishing, 1994.

Oja, Carol J. ed. *American Music Recordings: A Discography of Twentieth-Century US Composers.* New York: Institute for Studies in American Music, Brooklyn College, 1982.

Swafford, Jan. *The New Guide to Classical Music.* London: Macmillan Publishing Press Ltd, 1993.

The Gramophone Good CD Guide Harrow: General Gramophone Publications Ltd/QUAD, 1994.

March, Ivan, ed. *The Penguin Guide to Compact Discs and Cassettes.* Harmondsworth: Penguin Books, 1996.

The Penguin Guide to Bargain CDs and Cassettes. Harmondsworth: Penguin Books, 1994.

Mail order Companies:

Ladyslipper, UK and USA.
Leonarda Ltd. Co. New York, USA.
W. R. P. M., Birmingham, UK.

Index

Index